DISPLACEMENT:
Zweig, Roth and Benjamin

Three Eminent Writers Hunted to Death by Fascism

Richard Harper

ArrowGate

Published by Arrow Gate Publishing Ltd
London

16 15 14 13 12 11 10 9 8 7

Arrow Gate Publishing's titles may be purchased in bulk for educational,
business, fund-raising, or sales promotional use. For information,
please email info@arrowgatepublishing.com

A CIP catalogue record for this book is available from the British Library

ISBN 978-1-913142-44-5
eBook 978-1-913142-45-2

www.arrowgatepublishing.com

Arrow Gate Publishing Ltd Reg. No. 8376606
Arrow Gate Publishing 85 Great Portland Street, London. W1W 7LT

Arrow Gate Publishing Ltd's policy is to use papers that are natural, renewable
and recyclable products and made from wood grown in sustainable forests. The
logging and manufacturing processes are expected to conform to the environmental
regulations of the country of origin

Printed and bound by CPI Group (UK) Ltd, Croydon, CR0 4YY

Contents

To Amanda, Rebecca, Rupert, and Thomas

Introduction

This book describes the persecution, displacement and premature demise of three innocent victims of fascism: Stefan Zweig, Joseph Roth and Walter Benjamin. These three eminent Jewish writers, born towards the end of the 19th century and then having lived through the cataclysm of the First World War, had to navigate the deteriorating economic, social and political circumstances leading to the onset of the Second World War.

The following chapters describe the shared backgrounds and interactions between Zweig, Roth and Benjamin and how each sought unsuccessfully to survive the severe displacements that beset them. Zweig, Roth and Benjamin all died by suicide in exile. This work aims to evoke and understand how it must have felt to these men to be persecuted, exiled and subject to the fear of capture and death. This work seeks to understand too how and why this could have happened to them. After all, Zweig and Roth were well-known enough internationally for the news of their premature deaths to be prominently reported in the New York Times. It is similarly worth reflecting that Sigmund Freud, notwithstanding being internationally well-known, was persecuted, narrowly escaped capture and had to flee into exile in London at the age of 83 and as an invalid. To the fascists, age, health, professional accomplishments, and eminence meant nothing within the ordinary meaning of humanity.

At the end of the 19th century, Vienna enjoyed the golden era of Gustav Mahler, Gustav Klimt and Sigmund Freud. Stefan Zweig's passion for psychology and his friendship with Freud are considered in this book, as is Zweig's friendship with Theodore Herzl, the founder of the movement for a Jewish homeland. At the time, Vienna was the driving fulcrum of Jewish life and culture in Europe. However, the idyll of a city like Vienna was swept away by a rising tide of hatred, the scourge of endemic anti-Semitism, and then by the First World War. The philosopher Hannah Arendt described the issue as the 'Jewish question that had existed in German-speaking Central Europe since the 1870s and 1880s.' This book includes an examination of the 'Jewish question' and, by way of examples, contrasts on the one side Frederik Nietzsche's sister, Elisabeth Forster-Nietzsche, her husband Bernard Forster and Karl Lueger, the Mayor of Vienna, all leading antisemites at the time; with on the other side Alfred Dreyfus and Walter Rathenau foreign minister of Germany, two of the leading innocent victims of such hatred.

It is hard to fully take in the degree to which World War I shifted the tectonic plates of Europe as from 1918- four empires fell away: the German Empire, the Austro-Hungarian Empire, the Ottoman Empire, and the Romanov dynasty. While Zweig and Roth are more known for their fiction writing, they were also historians and peripatetic writers who directly described what they saw before them. In relation to Germany and Austria, Zweig's autobiography 'The World of Yesterday' transports the reader from the majesty of the Austro-Hungarian Empire as he saw it through to the sheer darkness of National Socialism. Zweig's 'Journeys', too, tells us directly what he saw on his travels to varying countries. Roth's essays in 'What I Saw- Reports from Berlin 1920-1933' give the reader a bird's eye view of everyday life in Berlin during the Weimar Republic, whilst the essays within his work 'Joseph Roth on the End of the World' chart mostly the period between 1933 and 1938, the era of National Socialism. Roth's work 'The Wandering Jews' and Zweig's work 'Journeys' reference first-hand the nature and extent of the displacement of Jews across Europe at the time. Walter Benjamin also wrote about his childhood, including his work 'Berlin Childhood around 1900' and provides a firsthand account of life as it was then in his home city.

The philosopher Hannah Arendt, in her seminal paper 'We Refugees', explores the extent of the burdens, fears and humiliations encountered by those displaced into exile, seeking only refuge and safety. She spoke partly from her own experience: she escaped from Gurs internment camp in southwestern France and fled to America from Portugal. All of this does not occur only to Jews and intellectuals; the pain, suffering and humiliation of displacement can and does inflict itself on many from anywhere. The following chapters seek to encapsulate the meaning and feeling of displacement suffered by whoever from wherever. Any further understanding, however small, that may come from reading this book of how it feels for any person to have to confront the fear and discontinuity of persecution and displacement will be a purpose well served.

CHAPTER 1
The Works of Zweig, Roth and Benjamin

THE WORKS OF STEFAN ZWEIG

Stefan Zweig wrote plays, poetry, biographies, an autobiography, translations, travelogues, and fiction. Growing up in Vienna, as Zweig did, the city was filled with cultural giants, including Mahler, Schoenberg, Klimt, Berg, and Sigmund Freud. The excellence of Zweig's writing matched his second-to-none ability to self-publicize, and that is why he was the most widely-read author of his day, with his works translated into at least 55 languages. In the 1920s and 1930s, he was the most translated writer in Europe. Even during the war years, when German writers were being shunned in the United States and Great Britain, Zweig's works received critical and public acclaim in those countries. He had become generally a very prominent figure in literary and societal terms.

In 1917, Zweig wrote a play called 'Jeremiah: A Drama in Nine Scenes.' Based on the life of the Prophet Jeremiah, it was written while he was still in military service and reflects his pacifist sentiments and Jewish background. It ends with the line: 'A people can never be put in chains, its spirit, never.' His full-length biographies include those of Marie Antoinette, Erasmus, Mary Queen of Scots and Frederik Nietzsche. The book 'Journeys' comprises Zweig's observations of his European travels.

His short stories/novellas came to dominate his fictional output. Zweig described the novella as an unfortunate format, too long for a newspaper or magazine and too short for a book. In his autobiography 'The World of Yesterday' Zweig says:

> *"I could not help wondering what exactly it was that made my books so unexpectedly popular... I think it arose from a personal flaw in me – I am an impatient, temperamental reader. Anything long-winded, high-flown or gushing irritates me, so does everything that is vague and indistinct, in fact, anything that unnecessarily holds the reader up... why not bring out a series of the great works of international literature, from Homer through Balzac and Dostoevsky to Mann's The Magic Mountain, with the unnecessary parts cut?"*

The novellas 'Letter from an Unknown Woman', which was made into a film in 1948, 'The Burning Secret', and 'Amok' depict characters in whom an uncontrollable and intense surge of emotions drives them forward. Other novellas include 'Compulsion', 'Fear'. and '24 Hours in the Life of a Woman'. Whilst 'The Burning Secret' was the most successful of his early short stories, the last one he wrote, 'The Royal Game', was also a success and one of Zweig's finest pieces of fiction. This novella is his only one to focus on the brutality and abuse of power by the Nazis. Zweig claimed that the destiny of his generation was 'loaded with the burden of fate as was hardly any other in the course of history.' This story, 'The Royal Game', conveys the impact of psychological terror and dictatorial rule, capturing the atmosphere of the time in an immensely haunting way.

Zweig wrote an incomplete novel entitled 'The Post Office Girl', which still merits reading. Zweig's only completed full-length novel is 'Beware of Pity'. This book is also one of his finest pieces of fiction. Nicholas Lezard, in his 2011 foreword to the book, writes:

> *"It is remarkable that Zweig only wrote one full-length novel....... 'Beware of Pity' is the length it is because it has to be and, as with all Zweig's writing, it zips along almost effortlessly like a clear running stream...."*

'Beware of Pity' was written in England in the 1930s and published in 1939 in Sweden, to where the German publishers had to move their business because of the Nazi regime in Germany. The Nazis were burning Zweig's books. Set in 1914, the novel is the story of a young Austrian cavalry officer, Anton Hofmiller, who befriends a local aristocratic millionaire, Kekesfalva and his family, particularly the older man's disabled daughter Edith, with terrible consequences. The book has many twists, turns and layers to it with much psychological nuance, with it transpiring that the aristocratic millionaire Herr Lajos von Kekesfalva is no aristocrat and was originally no nobleman or business magnate.

On page 145 of the 2011 publication of the book in English, the character Doctor Condor says to Anton Hofmiller:

> *"Well, we'd better begin at the beginning, and we can leave the aristocratic Herr Lajos von Kekesfalva right out of it at this point, for that gentleman didn't even exist yet. There was no owner of a large estate in a black coat and gold-rimmed glasses, no nobleman or business magnate. There was only a narrow-chested, sharp-eyed little Jewish boy in a poverty-stricken village on the border between Hungary and Slovakia. His name was Leopold Kanitz, but I believe he was generally known as Lammel Kanitz."*

One layer of the book then charts how this little Jewish boy becomes a millionaire and acquires an aristocratic title and a sizeable baronial estate from such humble beginnings. Another interesting aspect of the book is the insight it gives into the working life of an Austrian cavalry officer through the leading character, Anton Hofmiller.

It is also interesting to note that within the 2011 edition of Beware of Pity, the words of Stefan Zweig himself appear under the heading "Author's Note." Within such a short note, Zweig is meticulous in succinctly describing the standards and etiquettes of an Austrian officer of the Austro–Hungarian army.

"The World of Yesterday" is Zweig's autobiography/memoir. It is powerful and haunting. It will be referenced at differing points within this book. This is because we, readers, can hear Zweig's voice directly through it. Only days before his suicide, Zweig posted to his publishers in both Europe and America the manuscripts for "The Royal Game" and "The World of Yesterday." Zweig's short essays within his book 'Journeys' encompass the varying countries he visited between 1902 and 1940—concise and succinct, such essays too provide a fascinating historical insight.

Zweig's death marked the high point of his literary standing. From then on, appreciation of his work markedly lessened to the extent that he became a somewhat little-known name. That said, in recent years, there has been a renewed appreciation of the variety and boldness of his writing. The clarity of Zweig's writing is indeed always compelling. Zweig's important fiction and a number of his biographies have been reissued, and there have also been published translations of the incomplete novel, "The Post Office Girl", and of a long-lost novella entitled "Journey into the Past." It is accurate to say that Zweig wrote two novels: one complete, "Beware of Pity"; and one incomplete, "The Post Office Girl."

A book of Stefan Zweig's stories, 'Six Stories' translated by Johnathan Katz, has only recently been published.

The article on the book in the Times Saturday Review of 24 February 2024 by John Self is entitled 'The Genius Who Inspired Wes Anderson' and is sub-headed: 'These tales of passion and obsession remind us why Stefan Zweig was a bestseller in his day.' Zweig's writing inspired Wes Anderson's 2014 film The Grand Budapest Hotel.

The play 'Visit from an Unknown Woman' written by the internationally renowned playwright Christopher Hampton, is based on Stefan Zweig's short story 'Letter from an Unknown Woman' and received its English language premiere at Hampstead Theatre London in 2024 following a triumphant run in Vienna. Zweig has even permeated the world of classical music. Inspired by Zweig's memoir, which celebrates Viennese culture before the First World War, the internationally acclaimed pianist and composer Stephen Hough composed the piano concerto entitled 'The World of Yesterday.'

THE WORKS OF JOSEPH ROTH

This summary of Roth's writing commences with his two most recognisable novels 'Job: The Story of a Simple Man,' and 'The Radetzky March.'

In 1930, Roth published 'Job: The Story of a Simple Man,' which can be described as his most Jewish book; it is a fable of Jewishness and the story of Mendel Singer, his wife Deborah and their four children living within a strong Jewish community in the Austro-Hungarian Empire. Their three sons are Jonas and Shemariah, and the youngest is Menachim, who is a very disabled child; their one daughter is Miriam. The two eldest sons take distinctly different views concerning serving in the military. Jonas goes willingly to fight, and his whereabouts become unknown. Shemariah, on the other hand, deserts the army and escapes to America. There, he integrates and chooses to be known as Sam; he is successful in both his business and personal life. He marries and has a child. Mendel and Deborah are concerned that their daughter is 'going with Cossacks' and wish for her to be removed from that temptation. Mendel and Deborah face an agonising dilemma: they wish to make a new life, joining their son Sam in America and removing their daughter from her current temptations, yet their youngest disabled son is too incapacitated to be able to join them. They make the difficult decision to leave him behind. Mendel and his wife and daughter depart for America. They are pleased to be reunited with Sam, yet Mendel does not settle and longs for his original home in Europe. Matters deteriorate since the daughter Miriam becomes mentally ill, and Mendel's wife becomes sick. Sam is then called up by the USA military when war breaks out and is very willing to serve his new country, yet sadly dies in fighting in France. This grave blow means Mendel has lost Jonas and Sam in war and his wife and daughter to illness. Then, the miracle occurs. Menuchim tracks his father down in America, and it transpires that Menuchim has recovered from his serious physical incapacity and become a famous symphony conductor. They are reconciled, and Menuchim is willing to take his father back to visit his old home in Europe. Marlene Dietrich declared on its publication that her favourite novel was Roth's 'Job', a powerfully beautiful book.

In 1932, Roth's 'The Radetzky March' was published, one of the great novels about the Habsburg era. It is widely acknowledged to be a masterpiece. The novel charts the decline and collapse of the Austro-Hungarian Empire seen through the prism of three generations of the Trotta family. It is primarily set on the Empire's remote edges. It is a narrative that tracks through garrisons, brothels and bars in the Kingdom of Galicia, where Roth was born. The first-generation grandfather is an ordinary soldier who saves the emperor's life at the Battle of Solferino and is given the title of Baron. He disagrees with published descriptions of his actions at Solferino and does not wish his son to be a soldier.

The second generation, his son Baron Trotta, becomes District Commissioner- a senior civil servant- with a faithful servant, Jacques. The third generation, the District Commissioner's son, Lieutenant Trotta, is an officer in the army with a very formal relationship with his father, the District Commissioner. The Lieutenant firmly adheres to loyalty to Emperor Francis Joseph and proudly carries his grandfather's bravery at Solferino. Lieutenant Trotta moves to a regiment on the edge of the Empire, and it is there, literally and metaphorically, that he is in swampy terrain—he gets into various troubles, including gambling debts. His father uses his position and influence to see the emperor, who settles the son's debts. The son (Lieutenant Trotta) becomes disillusioned with army life and empire, retires to simple country living, and is content. His father foresees the breakup of the Empire. World War 1 breaks out, and he (the son) is recalled to the army in action. He goes to fetch a bucket of water for his men and is shot dead in the back of his head. The father (the District Commissioner) has now lost his loyal servant and son. He then sees the emperor die. He then dies, too.

Throughout the 1920s, Roth wrote prolifically, travelling incessantly throughout Europe on assignment as a journalist/correspondent. Roth wrote seventeen novels and novellas. His first unfinished novel, 'The Spider's Web', was serialised in an Austrian newspaper in 1923. In 1924, he published Hotel Savoy, which was translated into English. The book depicts prostitution, corruption, poverty, exploitation and agitation. His novels 'Rebellion' and 'The Spider's Web', together with 'Hotel Savoy', make up what is considered Roth's early period.

These were realistic novels about contemporary politics. There followed the works: 'Flight Without End', 'Zipper and His Father', and 'Right and Left' – all three novels were about soldiers coming home, only to discover they have no home to come back to.

Another much-overlooked aspect of Roth's writing is his non-fiction output. Roth was also an accomplished historian, as he travelled across Europe, describing peoples' everyday lives, thereby reflecting social, economic and political circumstances. In 1927, he published the short nonfiction book 'The Wandering Jews.' It is about the plight of the Jews in the mid-1920s who, with other refugees and displaced persons in the aftermath of World War 1 and the Russian Revolution, had fled to the West from Russia, Lithuania and Poland. In 1926, Roth visited the Soviet Union, and the final chapter of the 'Wandering Jews' is entitled 'The Condition of the Jews in Soviet Russia.' His collections of Essays entitled 'The Hotel Years' and 'Joseph Roth What I Saw Reports from Berlin 1920-33' provide a real insight into the realities of life in the Weimar Republic. There is also his collection of essays, 'Joseph Roth On the end of the world', written whilst he was exiled in Paris from 1933 until he died in 1939. There is not to be overlooked too, Roth's detailed and revealing correspondence as set out in 'Joseph Roth: A Life in Letters.'

Whilst 'The Radetsky March' marked the height of his fiction writing powers, Roth continued writing. He wrote his haunting Napoleon fantasy novel 'The Hundred Days.' He came to think little of this book, yet it is a novel of great sensitivity and resonance in which Roth turns his attention from one Emperor, Franz Joseph, to another, Napoleon Bonaparte, during the three months between Elba and Waterloo, the so-called 'Hundred Days.' In this novel, Roth addresses the twilight of another empire. His Napoleon is a vivid description of waning greatness. There was then Roth's own epitaph novella, 'The Legend of the Holy Drinker.' This work has been described as Roth's swan song: this is the story of Andreas, a homeless drunk who lives under the bridges of the Seine. The last line of the short story says, 'May God grant us all, all of us drinkers, such a good and easy death!' His final novel was, in fact, 'The Emperor's Tomb' (1938), in which the central character ponders the favourable life he led under the reign of the Habsburg Empire.

Roth's work disappeared after he died in 1939, but the first collected German edition of his novels appeared in 1956, bringing him back into currency. Interest in him and his work has grown steadily ever since.

THE WORKS OF WALTER BENJAMIN

Walter Benjamin was a literary critic and essayist, yet he was also much more. In the wider sense, it is hard to classify or categorise his writing. His polymathic intellectuality embraced a seemingly never-ending range of diverse subjects of interest. He was a prolific writer. As Stephen Zacks writes in his 1999 thesis on Benjamin, early on in his career, Benjamin had set himself the task of becoming recognised as the greatest critic of German literature. By the time of his permanent exile in early 1933, he had practically succeeded in this task. Benjamin wrote two books on German literature: 'The Concept of Art Criticism on German Romanticism' (1920) and 'The Origin of German Tragedy' (1928). When the philosopher Hannah Arendt introduced Benjamin to the American public in 1967, she quoted Benjamin's old friend Gershom Scholem, who had called Benjamin 'the only true critic of German literature.' In the early 1920s, Benjamin protested against the 'cult of Goethe' that he associated with the surge of German nationalism leading up to the First World War. Benjamin's essay on Goethe's 'Elective Affinities' printed in 1924, positioned him as a leading authority on Goethe, but since it was written as an attack on the reigning school of literary criticism in Germany, it had deleterious consequences for his academic career. He offended the followers of Stefan George, who was leading the celebration of Goethe and was the cultural representative of the Weimar Republic. It also is to be noted, in relation to any such academic career, that Benjamin failed in an academic thesis because of 'incomprehensibility' or 'obscurantism'. In Ben Mauk's article, 'Hannah Arendt was right: Walter Benjamin is "sui generis,"' he writes of Benjamin's essay on Goethe:

> *"What the writer Hugo von Hofmannsthal said of Benjamin's essay on Goethe still rings true: it was, and is, 'absolutely incomparable.' Hannah Arendt pointed out that his assessment was precisely the rub; the essay was literally incomparable."*

Benjamin's literary output includes two books of short essays: one entitled 'One-Way Street'; the other entitled 'Illuminations'. Both of these books of essays have within them the essays: 'Franz Kafka'; 'Picturing Proust/The Image of Proust'; 'The Task of the Translator'; and 'The Work of Art in the Age of Mechanical Reproduction'. 'One-Way Street' alone has within it the essays: 'One-Way Street', 'Hashish in Marseille', 'Surrealism', and 'Brief History of Photography'. 'Illuminations' alone has within it the essays: 'Unpacking My Library'; 'What is epic theatre?'; 'On Some Motifs in Baudelaire'; and 'Theses on the Philosophy of History'. All these topics evidence the extraordinary eclectic mix of subjects that Benjamin wrote on. As Stephen Zacks wrote in his thesis on Benjamin, the review by Frank Kermode of the book of essays 'Illuminations' in The New York Review of Books was entitled: 'The incomparable Benjamin.'

It is manifest that Benjamin was fascinated by Proust, Kafka, and Baudelaire. Apart from his roles as a literary critic and essayist, Benjamin was also a translator. He translated the works of Baudelaire and a part of Proust's 'A La Recherche du Temps Perdu.' Benjamin holds the distinction of being the first German to translate Proust. An article on Benjamin, titled 'Even the Dead Won't Be Safe,' published by the National World War II Museum in New Orleans, recounts:

> *"A zealous collector, Benjamin hunted and purchased tomes on a staggering array of topics: science fiction, fairy tales and children's books, Judaica, philology, physics, and theology, as well as novels and poetry."*

In the edition of 'Illuminations' published by Fontana Press in 1992 – there is a compelling and detailed analytic introduction to Benjamin's work by Hannah Arendt. Within it, she includes saying:

> *"From the Goethe essay on, quotations are at the centre of every work of Benjamin's. This very fact distinguishes his writings from scholarly works of all kinds in which it is the function of quotations to verify and document opinions, wherefore they can safely be relegated to the notes. This is out of the question in Benjamin. When he was working on his study of German tragedy, he boasted a collection of over 600 quotations very systematically and clearly arranged...."*

Benjamin was widely admired as an outstanding intellectual and thinker by other writers. In another chapter, this book examines the loyal band of Benjamin's creative friends, Gershom Scholem, Theodor Adorno, and Hannah Arendt, who later achieved wide renown. Bertholt Brecht was also a close friend but was already well-known and established as an eminent playwright. Benjamin had met: Martin Buber; Andre Gide; Heinrich Mann; and Rainer Maria Rilke. As is written in the article of 30 September 2020 entitled 'Even the Dead Won't be Safe: Walter Benjamin's Final Journey', Theodor Adorno, who has been described as a disciple of Benjamin, said of Benjamin:

"Everything which fell under the scrutiny of his words was transformed as though it had become radioactive." What stood out to Adorno was Benjamin's originality, and the way he was able to relate to his subject matter in a way that seemed beyond convention.

Benjamin was fascinated by art and culture in the broadest sense, including painting, film, photography and radio. As set out by Stephen Zacks, Benjamin began broadcasting on the radio in 1927 and, by 1929, began working regularly on this medium. Between 1929 and 1932, Benjamin performed over 80 radio broadcasts on stations in Berlin and Frankfurt, including radio plays and literary talks. It is helpful to turn first to his best-known essay, 'The Work of Art in the Age of Mechanical Reproduction.' Benjamin introduces the concept of the authentic 'aura' of the source of a piece of 'pure art', which may be lost by the act of its mechanical reproduction. As Erik Larsen writes in his analysis of Benjamin's essay:

> *"Benjamin acknowledges the reality of artistic reproduction throughout history, although he suggests that mechanical reproduction introduced an entirely new and revolutionary change in the experience of the artwork. With mechanical reproduction, which appears in its most radical forms in film and photography, millions of images of an original are circulated, all of which lack the 'authentic' aura of their source."*

It is worthwhile to reflect that Benjamin was exploring the nature and meaning of reproductive technology very early compared to others, given that this essay was published in 1936. By then, he had already become experienced in radio broadcasting. Benjamin was a pioneer and forward thinker in what may now be described as the 'modern media.' In their biography of Benjamin, Eiland and Jennings contend that:

> *"As a critic, Benjamin not only reshaped our understanding of many important writers, but he recognised the potentials and hazards of technological media that revolutionised culture during his lifetime."*

Benjamin's idea for an article on the Paris Arcades began on a walk with his friend Franz Hassel in 1926 when the latter was collaborating with him on translating Proust's work. The first Paris arcades, constructed early in the 19th century, sometimes enclosed several streets under a glass roof. What attracted Benjamin was the simultaneity of being both outside and inside, especially with the fashionable rows of shops with dazzling displays of commodities behind glass façades. Benjamin continued to work on 'The Arcades Project' as it became known for the rest of his life. It was a marathon project for him and remained unfinished up to the time of his death. It has been published unfinished and is an unusual and extraordinary work. It studied Paris's architecture and material culture in the 19th century. In the 1930s, Benjamin wrote a memoir entitled 'Berlin Childhood Around 1900.' It, too, remained unpublished during his lifetime. It is not a memoir in the customary sense. This work focuses not on persons or events but on places and things, all seen from a child's perspective. It, too, is an unusual and extraordinary work. In 1941, Benjamin's longstanding friend Gershom Scholem published his first major book, 'Major Trends in Jewish Mysticism', with the following dedication:

> *"To the memory of Walter Benjamin, the friend of a life-time whose genius united the insight of a metaphysician, the interpretive power of the Critic and the erudition of the Scholar died at Port Bou (Spain) ON HIS WAY TO FREEDOM."*

In the article 'Even the Dead Won't Be Safe: Walter Benjamin's Final Journey' dated 30 September 2020, it is said:

> *"Walter Benjamin (1892 – 1940) was one of the seminal critics of modern cultural life (literature, theatre, phil-osophy, theology, the study of language, the metropolis and its temptations and perils, painting, architecture, photography, radio, and the motion picture). Whilst it is disgraceful that he was never offered an academic pos-ition, typical scholarly boundaries and territorialism could not contain him. Benjamin's intellect was prodi-gious, restless and nomadic."*

Although widespread acclaim eluded Benjamin during his life, the decades following his death won his work posthu-mous renown. 'The Arcades Project,' the individual essay 'One Way Street' and his memoir on his childhood in Berlin exem-plify the complexity of Benjamin's writings, which transgress disciplinary borders and rules of genre. Although, as already indicated, Benjamin was a literary critic and essayist, beyond that, he can be described as a polymathic visionary and phi-losopher who wrote on a wide range of issues that are still prescient today. Of interest again is the article by Ben Mauk published in March 2014 entitled 'Hannah Arendt was right: Walter Benjamin is "sui generis."' Arendt – who introduced Benjamin to the American public in 1967 and much contrib-uted to his renaissance – has profoundly written:

> *"The trouble with everything Benjamin wrote was that it always turned out to be sui generis. Posthumous fame seems to be the lot of the unclassifiable ones, that is, those whose work neither fits the existing order nor introduces a new genre that lends itself to future classification."*

ZWEIG, ROTH AND BENJAMIN:

A COMPARATIVE OVERVIEW OF THEIR WRITINGS

Zweig, Roth and Benjamin were all contemporary men of letters. They were peripatetic, eminent and illustrious writers whose outputs were prolific. Zweig, Roth and Benjamin were writing alongside Austrian and German writers such as Thomas Mann, Hermann Hesse, Sigmund Freud and Bertolt Brecht. It is remarkable how much material Zweig, Roth, and Benjamin were able to produce at such a young age. This book does not seek to include references to all of their works. There is a strikingly similar preoccupation in the writing of Zweig and Roth with life in the Austro-Hungarian Empire, as exemplified in 'Beware of Pity' by Zweig and 'The Radetzky March' by Roth. Zweig and Benjamin were polymaths with seemingly unending interests, knowledge and understanding of many subjects. They (Zweig and Benjamin) had exquisite and extensive collections of varying artefacts. They were both highly esteemed within intellectual circles, and Zweig became a feted literary figure worldwide during his lifetime. Yet it was Roth who was able to write a seminal work, 'The Radetsky March'; his overall works, including the latter and 'Job: The Story of a Simple Man,' carry the weight and gravitas of Stendhal and Tolstoy. Zweig, for all his gifted, varied writings and wide-ranging societal contacts, could not write a work comparable to that of Joseph Roth or Thomas Mann. Zweig was aware of the possible limitations of the novella, his main fiction form, compared to the novel. It is appropriate that his work is being reassessed because, although he did not hit all the heights of Roth or Thomas Mann, Zweig has left a legacy of varied and prolific writing material of an outstandingly high quality. It is the effortless clarity of his writing that is so compelling. As for the work of Benjamin, it is virtually impossible to categorise the nature of his writing because he interweaves into his subject matter various intellectual disciplines: literary analysis, translation, history, philosophy, architecture, bibliography, autobiography, biblical study and the art of modern communications. Gershom Scholem described Benjamin as a great metaphysian and bibliophile. Benjamin's eclectic interests ranged from Marxism to mysticism. His Theses on the Philosophy of History include marrying Marxism with theology. To many, Benjamin is a visionary writer who could cross conventional literary and intellectual boundaries.

In contrast with the clarity, accessibility and consistency found in Zweig's writings, to others, Benjamin's work can be somewhat obtuse, impenetrable or unduly complex, as seen within his unfinished 'The Arcades Project.' That said, many contend with conviction that it was Benjamin who, well ahead of his time, foresaw the arrival of the modern age of media communications as seen within his essays 'Brief History of Photography' and 'The Work of Art in the Age of Mechanical Reproduction.' His works are unique and one of a kind; challenging unease can be created when it is difficult to place an artist. Benjamin's works continue to be increasingly fascinating, particularly to intellectuals. Perhaps it can be said that Benjamin was a genius of all trades and a master of none.

Finally, in relation to all three writers, there is importance in their nonfiction work. This emanates principally from Zweig's autobiography 'The World of Yesterday' and Zweig's

'Journeys' as well as Roth's compelling works: 'The Wandering Jews'; 'What I Saw Reports from Berlin 1920-1933'; 'The Hotel Years'; and 'Joseph Roth on the End of the World.' The correspondence in Joseph Roth's 'A Life in Letters' is significant in not only contributing to understanding Roth's character but also conveying the strengths and weaknesses of the long-standing friendship between Roth and Zweig. In relation to Benjamin, His work 'Berlin Childhood around 1900' too is a valuable but typically challenging historical remembrance of Berlin when he was very young.

CHAPTER 2

Zweig, Roth and Benjamin: Their Backgrounds

ZWEIG

Stefan Zweig was born in Vienna, Austria-Hungary, on 28 November 1881 and died on 22 February 1942. His was a family of great wealth. He was the son of Ida Breltauer, a daughter of a Jewish banking family and Moritz Zweig, a wealthy Jewish textile manufacturer. Stefan Zweig described himself as an Austrian, a Jew, an author, a humanist and a pacifist. In his autobiography "The World of Yesterday," Zweig emphasised: "I was sure in my heart from the first of my identity as a citizen of the world."

He studied philosophy at the University of Vienna and, in 1904, earned a doctoral degree with a thesis on 'The Philosophy of Hippolyte.' He spent a short period in Berlin, then returned to Vienna. His academic nature and the early successful publication of his poetry persuaded his parents that he should be excused from working in the family business. Zweig served in the Archives of the Ministry of War during World War 1. He married Friderike Maria von Winternitz (born Burger) in 1920. They lived in a beloved house in Salzburg. Zweig wrote prolifically and travelled widely and internationally. In Brussels, he befriended the French-Belgian poet Émile Verhaeren and immediately began translating his works; in Paris, he got to know Rainer Maria Rilke and Romain Rolland. He met Rodin, Yeats, Pirandello, Valéry, and many others. He and his wife divorced in 1938. They had no children. In the Chapter of his autobiography 'The World of Yesterday' entitled 'Detours on the Way to Myself', Zweig writes:

> *"My life was still governed in some odd way by the idea that everything was only temporary. Nothing that I did, I told myself, was the real thing—not in my work, which I regarded as just experimenting to discover my true bent, not the women with whom I was on friendly terms."*

Notwithstanding such doubts, he became an international success as a writer. Leaving Austria for England in 1934, he lived first in London, then from 1939 in Bath. In the late summer of 1939, Zweig married his new secretary, Elisabet Charlotte "Lotte" Altmann, in Bath, England. In 1940, Zweig and his wife set sail to America, where they lived for two months. On 22 August 1940, they moved again to Petropolis, a mountain town north of Rio de Janeiro, Brazil. The circumstances of the final demise of Zweig and his new wife can be seen in the description of their final journey later in this book.

ROTH

Joseph Roth's name upon birth was Moses Joseph Roth. He was born on 2 September 1894 and died on 27 May 1939. The place of his birth in 1894 was Brody, Austrian Galicia, near modern Ukraine. This was on the outskirts of the Austro-Hungarian Empire. At the time of Roth's birth, Brody was one of the seats of Central European Jewish civilisation, heavily populated by a growing middle class to which his own family belonged. Roth never knew his father, Nahum, who suffered from mental illness and vanished soon after his son's birth.

He was raised by his mother, Miriam. She was a cultured Jewess but somewhat overprotective and overbearing. Having graduated from the local gymnasium, Roth left Brody and went to the nearest large town, Lemberg (subsequently Lvov, USSR, now Lviv, Ukraine), where in 1913, he began his university studies before transferring to the University of Vienna to study philosophy and German literature. There, he dropped the word 'Moses' from his name and started to publish poems and articles. Roth was nineteen years of age and living in Vienna when Archduke Franz Ferdinand's assassination catapulted Europe into war. He was twenty-two years of age when Emperor Franz Joseph died and, as Roth himself put it, "an Epoque was buried." Roth's participation in World War 1 is considered later in this work. In 1920, Roth moved from Vienna to Berlin. This city became his main base for his journalistic and literary activities until 1933, when Hitler's seizure of power led him to have to leave Germany for France. Despite his distaste for Germany, the Weimar years were relatively good to him professionally. Jewish writers were still being published, cultural life was vibrant, and liberal newspapers provided an outlet for the young writer. In 1922, he married his girlfriend, Friederike (Friedl) Reichler, who soon developed signs of schizophrenia and eventually had to be institutionalised. As his world darkened, he threw himself into his work. His first (unfinished) novel, The Spider's Web, was serialised in an Austrian newspaper in 1923. In 1925, Roth was appointed Paris correspondent of the Frankfurter Zeitung. For this purpose, Roth and his wife moved to Paris, his favourite city. His writing was usually found in a part of the newspaper called the feuilleton – the part of the paper devoted to fiction, criticism or light literature. His style was urbane, sophisticated, witty and brief, writing in the style of a literary novel. Yet Roth was, at the same time, politically attuned to all of the seismic changes in the world. In 1928, Roth's wife had a total breakdown, and after that, she was placed in a psychiatric hospital in Vienna. As a renowned roving correspondent, Roth travelled to the South of France in 1925, to the Soviet Union in 1926, to Albania and the Balkans in 1927, and to Italy and Poland in 1928. On 30 January 1933, the day Hitler was named Reich Chancellor of Germany, Roth boarded a train from Berlin to Paris, never again to set foot in Germany.

BENJAMIN

Walter Benjamin was born on the 15 July 1892 in Berlin. His parents were Emil, a businessman, and his wife Pauline. They were Jewish but, like many others, not strictly observant. In the early 1930s, he wrote about his childhood in 'The Berlin Chronicle' and 'A Berlin Childhood Around 1900.' Benjamin was the first of three children. His brother Giorg was born in 1895, and his sister Dora in 1901. The family's circumstances were very comfortable indeed in material terms. His father had made his considerable fortune trading antiques and art. Benjamin came then from an upper-middle-class family. At school, he was taught by the educational reformer Gustav Wyneken, who was to fall into controversy. From 1912 to 1915, Benjamin carried on a peripatetic study of philosophy at the universities of Freiburg, Berlin and Munich. He also attended courses in art and literary history and other subjects, influenced by the sociologist and cultural historian Georg Simmel. Benjamin's girlfriend was Dora Kellner, who was married at that time. She initiated divorce proceedings, and in April 1917, she and Benjamin married and then moved to Switzerland. Their son Stefan Raphael was born on the 11 April 1918. Benjamin decided to work towards his degree in Bern, pursuing doctoral research into Kant and Romanticism. He had, too, a lively interest in experiences with hashish. He had no addiction whatever to drugs – this was simply a part of his never-ending thirst for learning about a variety of subjects, with this interest in the drug having arisen after he had read Herman Hesse's Steppenwolf. Other interests of Benjamin included the study of dreams and clairvoyance. On 27 June 2019, Benjamin passed his doctorate brilliantly. In March 1920, he, his wife, and his child returned to Germany to live with Benjamin's parents. They were no longer willing to fund his living costs, and throughout his career, Benjamin was beset by recurrent financial problems. In 1921, there were marital difficulties. Dora fell in love with Ernst Schoen, and Benjamin transferred his affection to Schoen's girlfriend, Julia Cohn. It was to her that Benjamin dedicated his essay on Goethe's 'Elective Affinities'. Benjamin and his wife patched up their marital difficulties and attempted to continue to live as man and wife, jointly caring for their son Stefan. Dora, his wife, suffered from a severe pulmonary disorder. In the summer of 1921, Benjamin accepted the offer to conceive and edit a magazine by the publisher who was set to produce his Baudelaire translations. The journal was to appear every three months. To ease his financial crisis, Benjamin bought books in markets and bookshops in one part of Berlin and sold them for a profit in another part of the city. Journalism was a source of income, and he pressed for publishing opportunities in literary journals. It is said that Benjamin hankered after an academic career. He would indeed have been much suited to that way of life. However, the academic studies he had submitted, which, if accepted, would have presaged an academic career, were rejected as incomprehensible and impenetrable. In 1923, he met Asja Lacis, a Bolshevik Latvian in Capri. In August 1925, Benjamin boarded a ship passing a raft of cities and alighted at Naples. He ended up in Riga, Latvia, to see Lacis. Benjamin returned to Berlin in December 1925. In March 1926, he set off for Paris, where he was translating Proust. He returned to Berlin in July 1926 to mark his father's death. He then soon returned to Paris. In September 1926, Benjamin completed his collection of essays entitled 'One-Way Street'. In December 1926, Benjamin went to Moscow for work and pleasure, and details of this visit are set out elsewhere in this book. He returned to Berlin in February 1927. In 1927, he began broadcasting on the radio. In the autumn of the same year, 1927, Benjamin went to Paris, and a new realm of study beckoned: a project to chart the Parisian Arcades and the world in which they existed. Benjamin was trying to realise a transformation within the disciplines of history and philosophy. In 1928, he experimented in Marseille with hashish stimulated by Hesse's novel, as indicated above. It was predictable that Benjamin's romantic dalliances and peripatetic travelling would end his marriage. In the late 1920s, there were bitter divorce proceedings; Dora alleged that Benjamin had failed to contribute to his son's upkeep and that he had slept with Lacis. She alleged that he was trying to take Stefan from her. Benjamin was now living on his own.

CHAPTER 3
Zweig, Roth and Benjamin: Their Suspicions of Nationalism

Joseph Roth was suspicious of all forms of nationalism. He reflected on these ideas in a letter dated October 1932, where he described the First World War and the collapse of the Austro-Hungarian Empire:

> *"The most powerful experience of my life and the end of my fatherland, the only one I have ever had."*

Sigmund Freud, who shared similar sentiments, wrote on Armistice Day 1918:

> *"I do not want to live anywhere else.... I shall live on with the torso and imagine that it is the whole."*

In his memoir 'The World of Yesterday', Zweig describes how lonely he felt in the first weeks of the First World War in 1914 when he became estranged from friends concerning the attitude to be taken towards the war. He says:

> *"Friends whom I had was known as inveterate individualists, even intellectual anarchists, became rabid patriots overnight, and from patriotism, they moved on to an insatiable desire to annex land...... Friends with whom I had never quarrelled in years accused me to my face of being no true Austrian anymore and said I should go over to France and Belgium."*

Roth's love for the Austro-Hungarian Empire and his manifest sorrow at its passing, particularly his warning about the dire consequences of the nationalism that would arise from this, are vividly reflected in his novel 'The Radetsky March.' One example only, emblematic of this, is an aristocratic character in the book, Count Chojnicki, who pronounces at one point to a party of guests:

> *"The monarchy is bound to end. The minute the emperor is dead, we shall splinter into a hundred fragments. The Balkans will be more powerful than we are. Each nation will set up its own dirty little government, even the Jews will proclaim a king in Palestine. The error has begun to stink of the sweat of democrats – I can't stand the Ringstrasse anymore. The workers all wave red flags and don't want to work anymore. The Mayor of Vienna is a pious shopkeeper. Even the parsons are going red, they've started preaching in Czech in the churches. At the Burgtheater, all the performances are filthy Jewish plays. Every week, another Hungarian water closet manufacturer is made a baron. I tell you, gentlemen, if we don't start shooting pretty soon, it'll be the end. You just wait and see what's coming to us."*

In his essay 'His K. and K. Apostolic Majesty' written in 1928 and included within his book 'The Hotel Years' Roth explains that a great part of his childhood and youth happened under the 'often merciless lustre of His Majesty', yet still he describes mourning the passing of his fatherland.

In his essay 'Journey through Galicia: People and Place' written in 1924 and included within his book 'The Hotel Years' Roth wrote:

> *"That's the way it was under Emperor Franz Joseph.... There are different uniforms, different eagles, different insignia. But the basic things don't change. Among these*

*basic things are: the air, the human clay, and God with
all His Saints that inhabit the heavens and whose images
are put up by the side of the road."*

Zweig, too, lamented the passing of the Austro-Hungarian
Empire and spoke of the corrosive poisoning of the mutilated
body of Europe from the end of the First World War onwards.
In his memoir 'The World of Yesterday, written in the late
1930s, Zweig says in this vein:

*"It will be decades before that other Europe can return to
what it was before the First World War. A certain gloom
has never entirely lifted from the once bright horizon of
the continent since then, and from country to country...
bitterness and distrust have lurked in the mutilated body
of Europe corroding it like poison. However much progress
in society and technology has been made... look closely
and there is not a single nation in our small Western
world that is not immeasurably worse off by comparison
with its old natural joie de vivre....... Can anyone imagine
an Austrian today as free and easy, as good-natured as he
would once have been, devoutly trusting in his Imperial
ruler and in God, who used to make his life so pleasant.......
we can bear witness that a carefree Europe once rejoiced
in a kaleidoscopic play of variegated colours. We tremble
to see how clouded, darkened, enslaved and imprisoned
the world has now become in its suicidal rage."*

In the early 1920s, Benjamin protested against the "cult of
Goethe" that he associated with the surge of German nationalism leading up to the First World War. Nietzsche, along
with Proust and Kafka, were seminally important influences on Zweig, Roth and Benjamin. Nietzsche, who died
in 1900, was prophetic in warning early on of what would
become so disastrous for humankind in the catastrophe

of the First World War. No one felt as keenly as Nietzsche "the augural cracking of the European edifice." No one felt as keenly as him that "an epoch was facing extinction."

Within Zweig's biography of Nietzsche is Nietzsche's prophetic phrase, found amongst his last writings:

"They will understand me after the next European war."

As set out in the biography, Nietzsche spoke of

"The nationalist heart pruritus (itch or irritation) and the blood poisoning of the peoples of Europe, cordoning them off from each other as if in quarantine." Nietzsche referred too to "The horned cattle nationalism."

Zweig writes in the biography:

"And the declaration of catastrophe issues with fury from his (Nietzsche's) lips, when he views the convulsive attempts to 'make permanent in Europe a network of small states,' merely to prop up a morality that rests only on business interests and commerce."

Zweig summed it up by saying: "This deadly crisis (an imminent European war) Nietzsche fatally sensed....in advance: that is his heroism and greatness."

It is necessary to reflect that Zweig, Roth, and Benjamin experienced the onset of two world wars, a severe and harsh burden for all those millions who shared these catastrophic events in one lifetime. From a bird's eye view, Zweig could significantly comment on the difference between those two experiences. In his memoir 'The World of Yesterday' he says:

"That was the difference. The war of 1939 had intellectual ideas behind it – it was about freedom and the preservation of moral values, and fighting for ideas makes men

hard and determined. In contrast, the war of 1914 was ignorant of the realities; it was still serving a delusion, the dream of a better world, a world that would be just and peaceful. And only delusion, not knowledge, brings happiness. That was why the victims went to the slaughter drunk and rejoicing, crowned with flowers and wearing oak leaves on their helmets, while the streets echoed with hearing and blazed with light, as if it were a festival."

CHAPTER 4

Zweig, Roth and Benjamin: Their Jewish Identities

ZWEIG

Zweig was a secular, assimilated Jew alienated from other Jews, especially the Ashkenazim from Eastern Europe, with their long kaftans, shawls and side locks, with whom he was now identified and with whom he had "no shared faith". In his memoir 'The World of Yesterday' Zweig wrote:

> "In Vienna I still felt tied to my environment. The literary colleagues with whom I mingled almost all came from the same middle-class Jewish background as I did; in a small city where everyone knew everyone else, I was inevitably the son of a good family, and I was tired of what was considered good society; I even like the idea of decidedly bad society, an unconstrained way of life with no one checking up on me."

Zweig said that his mother and father were Jewish only through accident of birth. Religion did not play a central role in his education. Yet Zweig never renounced his Jewish faith, was proud of being a Jew and wrote repeatedly on Jewish themes. In 1917, he wrote the play 'Jeremiah', previously described in this book. 'The Buried Candelabrum' is Zweig's only work of fiction depicting a Jewish religious world. It was written by him in exile from the Nazis and speaks to the plight of the

Jewish people. The story reflects Zweig's growing empathy with Jewish history and tradition, shared by many persecuted Jews in the 1930s. Zweig tells a story of the Menorah, a sacred multibranched candelabrum used in Jewish worship, being stolen and the expectation of the Jewish community upon the main character. This older man has become a rabbi, and he may be able to achieve a miracle of recovering it. The story is about a plea and desire for redemption—the older man's search and hope to find the Menorah will keep his people united and give them strength to face adversity.

'Buchmendel' is a 1929 short story telling the true story of an eccentric but brilliant book peddler, Jakob Mendel, who spends his days trading in one of Vienna's many coffeehouses. The Poland-born Russian Jewish immigrant is not only tolerated, but he is liked. In Zweig's novel 'Beware of Pity' comes the revelation that the aristocrat Herr Lajos von Kekesfalva, living in a large baronial estate, was not at all a nobleman. Rather, in origin, he was only a little Jewish boy in a poverty-stricken village on the border between Hungary and Slovakia. His name was Kanitz, and he was generally known as Lammel Kanitz. A central feature of the book is how such a major transition occurred. Jewishness was a part of Zweig's identity, as seen above in his writing. Yet, overall, this refined, polite, grand man of letters, a connected cosmopolitan, believed himself to be an internationalist, a European, a citizen of the world.

ROTH

Roth was a secular, non-practising Jew who came from Brody in Galicia, an entrenched centre of Jewish culture and religion at the time, where he was born. In Roth's childhood, over 70% of the town was Jewish. As Keiron Pim writes in his biography of Roth entitled 'Endless Flight: The Life of Joseph Roth,'

"The town became known as the Polish Jerusalem, and three times a day, three-quarters of Brody's population turned to face the real Jerusalem and pray."

A part of the process of transforming himself to become a secular Jew and to shed the orthodoxy of the religious environment he had grown up in was his decision to change his name- as indicated previously, he was born Moses Joseph Roth and dropped his first name Moses to become known simply as Joseph Roth. In later years, Roth described himself as a Catholic, yet he never renounced his Jewish identity. Jewishness was, to him, an irreplaceable talent or gift. He described Yiddish as 'the fate-speech of the Jews.'

In his first year as a Viennese journalist, from April 1919, Roth wrote one hundred and forty pieces for Der Neue Tag, many under the pseudonym Josephus. Keiron Pim, in his biography of Roth, reads this as an allusion to Flavius Josephus, the ancient Jewish historian of the disastrous war of 66–70 C.E., which led to the Jews being dispossessed both of Jerusalem and of the individual state re-founded by the Maccabees. Roth's wish to use such a pseudonym in a way speaks for itself.

Roth's works and writing evidence his continuing preoccupation with and attachment to Jewish faith and culture. "The Wandering Jews" is a powerful non-fiction evocation of the plight of the Jews during the period of the Weimar Republic. 'Job: The Story of a Simple Man' is a powerful and poignant novel deriving from the biblical story of Job. Moreover, there were Roth's friendships too. He retained close friendships with Stefan Zweig and Ernst Toller, both Jews. From Roth's body of work, both fiction and non-fiction, as well as his detailed correspondence with Zweig, came Roth's understanding that the fact of his Jewishness was determining the burning of his books by the fascists and the exile and persecution he was suffering. Indeed, Roth was proactive in telling other Jews, including Zweig, of the seriousness of the Jewish predicament and the likely imminent catastrophe of Jewish destruction by the Nazis: in this restricted sense only, Roth can be seen as a Jewish community leader assuming a responsibility to warn other Jews of what was to come.

BENJAMIN

Benjamin was an assimilated secular, non-practising Jew. He did not conceal his Jewish identity. Far from it, he understood himself to be a Jew and to be known as a Jew. He did not subscribe to organised religion and was mistrustful of religious and political institutions. Benjamin can be described as more of a Jewish thinker, and in an article entitled 'Benjamin's Displaced Jewish Tradition' Brian Britt writes:

> *"Far from passively inheriting Jewish tradition, Benjamin theorises the inheritance of tradition. This inheritance can be framed in terms of displacement, the shifting and transformation of religious beliefs and practices he identifies in his early and late writings. Drawn from Freud and Benjamin, the idea of displacement means that traditions change rather than go away, but the inheritance of tradition does not conform to simple grand narratives of decline, progress, or eternal recurrence."*

Among Benjamin's multifarious intellectual curiosities was his interest in the Bible and theology. Whilst he was subject to the influences of many other intellectuals, including Berthold Brecht, Benjamin was seminally influenced by the works of Kafka and Proust. The latter two iconic writers feature as significant subjects for analysis in his books of essays entitled "Illuminations" and "One-Way Street." Whilst Kafka was indisputably Jewish, there is contention about Proust's identity in this context. Proust was raised Catholic, but his mother, Jeanne Weil, was Jewish. Their bond was intense, and his mother's death in 1905, when Proust was 36, marked the beginning of his retreat into seclusion. Proust, a significant figure in world literature, fully supported Emil Zola's campaign to prove the innocence of Alfred Dreyfus. The relevance of this is that Benjamin was much taken not only by the brilliance of the writing of Kafka and Proust but also by the cultural Jewish influence of their thinking and work. Benjamin's close friends included Gershom Sholem, Theodor Adorno, Hannah Arendt, and Bertolt Brecht. Aside from Brecht, these friends also exposed Benjamin to Jewish culture, influence, and milieu.

CHAPTER 5

Rabid Antisemitism at the turn of the 20ᵗʰ Century

By the end of the 19th century and in the early years of the 20th century leading to the onset of World War 1, antisemitic hatred was endemic and rabid across Europe, but particularly so within Germany and the Austro-Hungarian Empire. Hannah Arendt's Introduction to the book of essays by Walter Benjamin entitled 'Illuminations' refers to 'what had since the 1870s or 1880s been called the Jewish question and existed in that form only in the German-speaking Central Europe of those decades'. There were two conflicting currents towards the Jews in Germany and within the Austro-Hungarian Empire. One was the seemingly widespread and welcomed fruitful and successful integration of Jews into the fabric of society. The word 'welcomed' is used because many Jews living within the Austro-Hungarian Empire, including Roth and Zweig, felt at home and protected by the emperor whose territories necessarily incorporated a diverse range of cultures and ethnicities. The other was the escalating and unchecked spread of vitriolic antisemitism to the extent that, as can be seen from the commentaries on the Forsters and Karl Lueger below, it became commonly acceptable within civic society to pronounce antisemitic views and distribute racist literature openly. Hannah Arendt, in her introduction to Benjamin's 'Illuminations,' refers to an article written by Moritz Goldstein in 1912 entitled 'German-Jewish Mt. Parnassus' and then examines head-on the insoluble nature of the answer to what she had described as the long-standing 'Jewish question':

"According to Goldstein, the problem as it appeared to the Jewish intelligentsia had a dual aspect, the non-Jewish environment and assimilated Jewish society, and in his view, the problem was insoluble. With respect to the non-Jewish environment, 'We administer the intellectual property of the people which denies us the right and ability to do so.' And further: 'It is easy to show the absurdity of our adversaries' arguments and prove that their enmity is unfounded. What would be gained by this? That their hatred is genuine. When all calumnies have been refuted, all distortions rectified, and all false judgments about us rejected, antipathy will remain as something irrefutable. Anyone who does not realise this is beyond help.' It was the failure to realise this that was felt to be unbearable about Jewish society, whose representatives, on the one hand, wished to remain Jews and, on the other, did not want to acknowledge their Jewishness..."

Joseph Roth also examines head-on what has been called the Jewish question in his work 'The Wandering Jews'. As Michael Hofmann says in his March 2000 preface to the book:

"The Wandering Jews does two things: it describes, as Roth says, the human beings who constitute the 'Jewish problem', and it casts about for a solution to that problem. In the first, it succeeds magnificently... So far as offering 'solutions' to the 'problem', that is a different matter.... What is left for Roth – and this is not a solution at all – is the destiny of the wanderer ('no home any-where, but their graves may be found in every cemetery').

In short, The Wandering Jews describes a problem that is not really a problem at all – more a blessing – and to which there is no solution. As one reads the 1937 preface, one senses that all Roth is able to hope for – and this is simultaneously a cause of his greatest despair – is conditions for Jews getting steadily and bearably worse. What happened instead was the Holocaust."

Roth's very own words in his preface to the 1937 edition of 'The Wandering Jews' provide at least three direct answers towards resolution of what has been called 'the Jewish question', albeit those direct answers are ones of pessimism.

The first answer he writes is Zionism, which:

"can bring only a partial solution to the Jewish question."

The second answer he writes is:

"Jews will only attain complete equality, and the dignity of external freedom, once their 'host nations' have attained their own inner freedom, as well as the dignity conferred by sympathy for the plight of others."

The third answer he writes is:

"It is- failing some divine intervention – hardly possible to believe that the 'host nations' will find such freedom and such dignity."

It is helpful to introduce what follows now. The Forsters and Karl Lueger, on the one side, represent and reflect, by way of examples only, the open and vitriolic antisemitic hatred during this period. Alfred Dreyfuss and Walter Rathenau, on the other side, represent and reflect, by way of examples only, two well-known and entirely innocent victims of such antisemitic hatred at that time.

ELISABETH NIETZSCHE-FORSTER AND BERNHARD FORSTER

Elisabeth Nietzsche-Forster was the sister of the philosopher Frederik Nietzsche. She was born in 1846, and when she died in 1935, Hitler attended her funeral. In his 1991 book "Forgotten Fatherland: The Search for Elisabeth Nietzsche" by Ben Macintyre, he writes of Elisabeth Nietzsche:

> *"Her ideas foreshadowed one of the darkest periods of human history.... but for more than 40 years she enjoyed fame and wealth as one of Europe's foremost literary figures; no woman, except perhaps Cosimo Wagner, was more celebrated in the cultural world of prewar Germany. She died just at the moment when people who shared many of her views were about to plunge Europe into devastating war and unleash the Holocaust of European Jewry."*

Elisabeth Nietzsche Forster, together with her husband, Bernhard Forster, were outspoken antisemites and Nazi sympathisers. Bernhard Forster described Jews as constituting a 'parasite on the German body.' Born in 1843, he set up in 1881 the far-right German People's League. Elisabeth Nietzsche is renowned for having distorted her brother Frederik's life work after he died in 1900, including completing untrustworthy and unreliable biographies of him. She and her husband, Bernhard Forster, are renowned as a couple for their failed attempt to create a new Fatherland called 'Nueva Germania', a purely Aryan colony in South America. They assembled twelve to fourteen German families who were supposed to become the nucleus of a strictly Aryan empire in South America. Elisabeth Nietzsche and Bernhard Forster, together with these German families, travelled to Paraguay from Hamburg in February 1886.

The colonial settlement was located in the jungles of Paraguay. Here, there was to be an Aryan settlement, an idyllic utopia for a pure and superior race. The settlers faced, in reality, an extremely harsh and unyielding environment in a remote and wild territory. The brave new world the couple envisaged never materialised. It was a failed racial experiment. Bernhard Forster, drinking heavily and in debt, became depressed and committed suicide on 3 June 1889. Elisabeth Nietzsche-Forster returned to Germany to care for her ailing brother Frederik, who was sinking deeper and deeper into madness. Frederik Nietzsche had long disapproved of his sister's anti-Semitism and had refused to have anything to do with her racist colony in Paraguay. Back in Germany, she, Elisabeth, had two purposes in mind. She sought to salvage her deceased husband's reputation by portraying him as a hero in a book entitled 'Bernard Forster's Colony New Germany in Paraguay' published in 1891. More disturbingly, she set about making herself a custodian of her brother Frederik's affairs, determined to turn him into the focus of the occult, enabling the Nazi regime to distort the essence of Nietzsche's work for their own propaganda purposes.

KARL LUEGER

Karl Lueger, who ran Vienna from 1897 until he died in 1910, was a formidable and divisive figure in the years leading up to the First World War and the collapse of the Austro-Hungarian empire. Lueger was first elected Mayor of Vienna in 1895, but this was still during the days of the Habsburg Monarchy, which meant that the emperor had to confirm the mayor to his office. The emperor at the time, Kaiser Franz Joseph, was much at variance with Lueger's personal and political views and refused to confirm him to the office for two years. The emperor only relented after an intervention by Pope

Leo X111, who gave Lueger his blessing. With his election as Mayor of Vienna in 1897, anti-Semitism reached its climax and became a social and political force dominating society. As may be seen from Peter Pulzer's 1964 'The Rise of Political Antisemitism in Germany and Austria', in Karl Lueger's speech on 2nd October 1897, he included saying:

> *"For my part, I like to ignore the small differences which might exist between one or other of the parties about the method of the struggle. I have very little regard for words and names and much more for the cause. Whether Democrat or anti-Semite, the matter really comes to one and the same thing. The Democrats, in their struggle against corruption, come up against the Jews at every step, and the anti-Semites, if they want to carry out their economic programme, have to overcome not only the bad Jews but the bad Christians also. All my party comrades share my opinion it is the first duty of a Democrat to take the side of the poor, oppressed people and to take up the fight with all determination against the unjustified and even harmful domination of a small fraction of the population..."*

Hitler, who spent part of his youth in Lueger's Vienna before the First World War, extolled the city Mayor in Mein Kampf as "the greatest German Mayor of all times." Lueger used anti-Semitism as a political instrument for mobilising the masses. His populist rhetoric stereotyped Jews as outsiders, differentiating them from the Viennese community. His cynical and chilling claim was: "I determine who is a Jew." He stoked both religious and economic antisemitism. In relation to the spiritual aspect, he made use of the popular myths of Christian anti-Jewishness that had been passed down over centuries and supported by official church doctrine. Concerning the economic aspect, he perpetuated the myth that Jewish industrialists and bankers were the cause of all social problems. What has made Lueger a divisive figure for Vienna's population is the modernity that he brought as Mayor to the structure of Vienna, overseeing the provision of the basis of contemporary Viennese services- energy and water supply networks and public transport systems. There has been, in recent times, a reappraisal in Austria of Lueger's legacy. In his article of the 27 April 2012, Ian Traynor for The Guardian newspaper sets out the words of the columnist Hans Rauscher:

> *"Lueger's legacy lives on in Vienna 100 years later. And so does his evil legacy-racism, demagoguery, xenophobia and the anti-Semitism that was his central political message. He gave the Viennese clean, fresh water. He also gave them the poison potion of a policy of hatred."*

ALFRED DREYFUS

The Dreyfus Affair was a political and criminal justice scandal in France from 1894 to 1906. The injustice to Dreyfus has become infamous. An artillery officer, Alfred Dreyfus, of Jewish descent, was convicted in 1894 of passing military secrets to the Germans. He was sentenced to life in prison. The affair revealed growing antisemitism across Europe. In 1896, evidence arose that a French Army major named Ferdinand Walsin Esterhazy was responsible for Dreyfus' alleged crimes. In 1898, Esterhazy was court-martialled and found not guilty. He later fled the country.

After Esterhazy's acquittal, a French newspaper published an open letter titled "J'accuse...!" by the well-known author Emile Zola, in which he defended Dreyfus and accused the military of a major cover-up in the case. As a result, Zola was convicted of libel, although he escaped to England and later managed to return to France. Amongst those who lent their weight to Zola's campaign was Marcel Proust, the greatest of French modernist writing. In a letter at the end of his life, Proust proudly recalled that he was the first of the "Dreyfusards." The strength of Proust's defence of Dreyfus has suggested to some that the importance of Proust's Jewish identity to understanding him and his writing is overlooked.

In 1899, Dreyfus was court-martialled for a second time and found guilty. The Dreyfus affair deeply divided France, not just over the fate of the man at its centre but also over a range of issues, including politics, religion and national identity. Dreyfus was pardoned by the French president days after the guilty verdict in the second trial. It was not until 1906 that Dreyfus was ultimately exonerated and reinstated to the French army. However, his case remained a notable example of antisemitism in the French criminal justice system, evidencing the way the press and public opinion can potentially distort a criminal case. After Dreyfus's exoneration in 1906, Marcel Proust wrote in dismay to a friend:

> *"To think this could have happened in France and not among the Apaches (a slang Parisian term for criminal gangs). The contrast that exists on the one hand between the culture, the intellectual distinction, and even the glitter of the uniforms of these people and their moral infamy is frightening."*

The Dreyfus affair convulsed not only France but a much wider audience. Theodor Herzl, the founder of the movement for a return of the Jewish people to their own homeland, was undoubtedly one of those so convulsed. As Henry J. Cohn sets out in his article entitled 'Theodor Herzl's conversion to Zionism':

> *"On January 5, 1895, Theodor Herzl witnessed the military degradation of Alfred Dreyfus. On May 14, 1895, the City*

Council of Vienna chose as its mayor Karl Lueger, leader of the anti-Semitic party of United Christians; Austria was plunged into political crisis for over a year, while confirmation of this appointment by the emperor remained in the balance. About the beginning of May 1895, Herzl was seized by the idea, which led him early in June to begin composing his book, the Jewish State, in which he proposed the organised exodus of Jews to an autonomous territory of their own, not necessarily Palestine. Standard accounts of his sudden conversion to this Zionist solution for the Jewish problem stress the immediate shock of the trial and condemnation of Dreyfus but underestimate the background of virulent anti-Semitism in Herzl's adopted hometown, Vienna. This article seeks to reverse the emphasis in evaluating the tangled skein of motives influencing the founder of Zionism."

In 1899, in an article intended for publication in the US, Herzl wrote that the Dreyfus Affair made him a Zionist.

WALTER RATHENAU

In 1922, Walther Rathenau became the first Jew to serve as Germany's foreign minister—and was assassinated by the far right six months later. Rathenau had been educated as an engineer and became experienced as an executive officer of his family's electrical company, AEG. In 1918, Rathenau wrote in his essay 'State and Judaism: A Polemic' that:

"Early in life, every German Jew will experience a painful moment which he remembers all his life: when for the first time he becomes fully aware that he has entered the world as a second-class citizen and that no amount of hard work and no merit can free him from this position."

During the last half of World War I, Rathenau directed the Raw Materials Department in the German Ministry of War. He represented the new German Weimar Republic at various diplomatic and treaty negotiations. He was on the German delegation at Versailles in 1919 and negotiated the Rapallo Treaty with the Soviet Union in 1922. He then became Germany's foreign minister in 1922, the first Jew to hold a cabinet post in Germany. Rathenau won some reparations concessions from the victors of World War I and generally improved relationships between Germany and her former enemies. A strong German patriot, he remained a liberal democrat and advocated socially minded policies to moderate the capitalist economy.

As a Jew and a committed advocate of the Weimar Republic, Rathenau was a lightning rod for the hatred of those on the conservative and radical right who despised the Weimar Republic and hated Jews. Among the hateful slogans written about him was the following: "Erschlag den Walter Rathenau/ die gottverdammte Judensau" ('Slay that Walter Rathenau/ the goddamned Jewish sow'). In his autobiography 'The World of Yesterday, Stefan Zweig spoke of his friendship with Rathenau:

> *"Our friendship was warm and of long-standing... Busy as he was, he always had time for a friend. I saw him in the most desperate days of the war, and just before the conference of Genoa, and few days before his assassination, I drove with him in the very car in which he would be shot taking the same route as he did that day.... I seldom felt the tragedy of the Jewish identity more strongly than I did in him. In spite of his obvious distinction, he was full of profound uneasiness and uncertainty. My other friends, for instance, Verhaeren.... were a bit not one-tenth as clever nor one-hundredth as knowledgeable and experienced as he was, but they were sure of themselves."*

The two far-right gunmen who murdered Rathenau as he drove to his office from his home in Berlin were former officers, Erwin Kern and Hermann Fischer, while the far-right driver of their car, Ernst Werner Techow, was 20 years old. Ambushing Rathenau's chauffeur-driven limousine, the killers sprayed the minister with bullets and lobbed a grenade into his car. His spine and jaw shattered, and Rathenau died in minutes. Even his killers were aware that Rathenau was a man of exceptional qualities. Yet, they also believed he was one of the Elders of Zion, the mythical cabal of Jews who, according to the notorious Protocols forgery, were secretly conspiring to rule the world.

CHAPTER 6

The Participation (or otherwise) of Zweig, Roth and Benjamin in World War 1

ZWEIG

In his autobiography "The World of Yesterday", Zweig describes how, at 32 years old, he was rejected for military service in World War 1, being declared unfit for it. There were penalties in Austria at the time for conscientious objectors, so he looked around for something he could do without being involved in any violent activity. One of his friends, a high-ranking military officer who worked in the War Archive, helped him to get a post there. Zweig's job was to act as a librarian. As the military situation worsened, more and more of those around him were called up to the front. Oliver Matuschek, in his biography of Zweig entitled "Three Lives", carefully sets out the strings Zweig pulled to get to Switzerland and to stay there until the end of the war.

ROTH

When World War I broke out, Roth was a literature student in Vienna. In his essay 'Where the World War Began' written in 1927 and included in Roth's book 'The Hotel Years', he writes:

> *"The World War began in Sarajevo, on a balmy summer afternoon in 1914. It was a Sunday; I was a student at the time. In the afternoon, a girl came around.... In her straw hat was a telegram, the first special edition I had seen, crumpled and terrible, a thunderbolt on paper. 'Guess what', said the girl,' they've killed the heir to the throne...'"*

In 1916, Roth left university in Vienna and volunteered to serve in the Imperial Habsburg Army fighting on the Eastern Front. He had a modest administrative desk job whose benefit, from Roth's point of view, was that it was about 10 kilometres from the front line, away from any action that could endanger him. In his 1928 essay entitled 'His K and K. Apostolic Majesty' included within the book 'The Hotel Years' Roth writes of his presence at the funeral of Emperor Franz Joseph, who died on 21 November 1916:

> *"When he was buried, I stood, one of the many soldiers of his Viennese garrison, in my new field grey uniform that we were to go to war in a few weeks later, a link in the long chain that lined the streets. The shock that came from understanding the day was an historic one encountered a complicated sadness about the passing of a fatherland that had raised its sons to opposition. Even as I was condemning it, I already began to mourn it. While I bitterly measured the proximity of the death to which the dead Emperor was sending me, I was moved by the ceremony with which his Majesty (and this was Austria–Hungary) was being carried to the grave. I had a clear sense of the absurdity of the last years, but this*

absurdity was also part of my childhood. The chilly sun of the Habsburgs was being extinguished, but it had at least been a sun."

Roth later was, at best, disingenuous and, at worst, dishonest about his activities and role in the war. He claimed to have been an Austrian officer who had won medals for distinguished service and that he had been a prisoner of war in Russia and then escaped. None of that was true. During the war, he began drinking heavily for the first time.

BENJAMIN

Austria–Hungary declared war on Serbia on July 28, 1914, beginning World War I. On 8 August 2014, two of Benjamin's friends, Fritz Heinle and his partner Rika Seligson, committed suicide in Berlin. Heinle was just 19. He was a poet. Benjamin was very much an admirer and friend of Heinle. Rika was the sister of Carla Seligson, a very close colleague of Benjamin's in the youth movement. The way the suicide was carried out is described by Martin Jay in his article "Walter Benjamin, Remembrance, and the First World War":

"Their act, carried out by turning on the gas, was designed as a dramatic protest against the war, a war in which lethal gas was, as we know, to take many more victims. Benjamin learned of the news when he was awakened by an express letter from Heinle with the grim message, 'You will find us lying in the meetinghouse.'"

Benjamin was deeply distressed and disturbed by this news. That same month (August 2014), he volunteered for the Kaiser's army, but the military authorities refused him. In the autumn of 1914, Benjamin was called up a second time.

Benjamin, this time, was able to fake palsy. In her book on the life of Benjamin entitled "Critical Lives," Esther Leslie describes how Benjamin managed to do this:

> *"War once again impressed itself on Benjamin. Scholem aided him in his efforts to evade war when he was summoned a second time. The two stayed up until 6 am drinking black coffee on the 20/21 October. There was much to discuss: philosophy, Judaism, Kabbalah, politics – and the next day, Benjamin presented himself as an undesirable soldier to the authorities and was deferred for another year."*

In January 2017, Benjamin was again ordered to report, and this time, his wife, Dora Kellner, hypnotised her husband, enabling Benjamin to be able to simulate the symptoms of sciatica. Benjamin avoided conscription, and soon after, he and Dora left Germany for Switzerland.

CHAPTER 7
Displacement of Persons in Weimar Berlin

What is so striking about Zweig's memoir 'The World of Yesterday' is his rich evocation of Vienna's well-to-do and thriving turn-of-the-century culture. Zweig describes the city where he grew up and eventually became so well-known as the Vienna of the educated Jewish bourgeoisie. He paints a detailed picture of Vienna's golden age in or about 1900. Such a boisterous and confident culture within that City at that time is, however, in marked contrast to the fragility, struggles and decline of the Weimar Republic, established in 1919 at the end of the First World War and which reached its demise with Hitler's seizure of power in 1933.

Michael Hofmann, in his preface to Roth's book 'The Wandering Jews' writes:

"In the early 1920s, as a young journalist in Vienna and then in Berlin, Roth wrote numerous articles drawing attention to the awful plight of refugees and displaced persons- Jews and others- in the aftermath of World War I, the Russian Revolution, and the redrawing of national frontiers following the Treaty of Versailles (1919). Hundreds of thousands of people – those lucky ones who had not been butchered already – found themselves unhoused and persecuted, with no option but to take to the road. They sought shelter in cities and towns where most of

them had never been and, unfortunately, where they were made despicably unwelcome."

Roth's important work, "What I Saw Reports from Berlin 1920 to 1933," captures the everyday life of 1920s Berlin. His reports portray the daily lives of Berliners, particularly the forgotten: displaced persons, Jewish immigrants, the nameless dead, bathhouse denizens, and criminals. Part 11 is entitled 'The Jewish Quarter' and contains reports including those entitled 'Refugees from the East', 'Solomon's Temple in Berlin' and 'The Wailing Wall.' Part 111 of the book is entitled 'Displaced Persons' and contains reports as follows: 'With the Homeless' (1920); 'The Steam Baths at Night' (1920; 'Nights in Dives' (1921); 'Schiller Park' (1923); and 'The Unnamed Dead' (1923). The book overall conjures up Berlin's moral bankruptcy, its debauched beauty and the rising danger of the Nazi party that would ultimately drive Roth into exile. Germany seemed a place without hope: in 1923, there was hunger in the city, and the train network was collapsing. In his book of essays entitled 'The Hotel Years,' Roth writes of Germany's widespread hunger and unemployment. In his 1923 essay 'Germany in Winter', he writes:

> *"But.... the station guard goes hungry, trains come and go unpunctually, the heating doesn't always work, the porters haggle, the toilets don't flush, and the lighting in the compartments is wretched. Whereas, in Germany, railway carriages are full of embittered businessmen, and a hungry inspector checks your tickets..."*

In May 1923, there was dizzying hyperinflation. Roth provides a fascinating insight into the severe monetary difficulties he encountered in an essay written in January 1924 entitled

'The Currency-Reformed City', also included within 'The Hotel Years'. In the essay, he writes:

"The only affordable currency reformed city in Germany is Hamburg. It has introduced its own currency, the much praised, much sought after Hamburg Gold Mark, which sells at a premium on the black market. I have seen one for myself, a Hamburg Gold Mark, it's a little scrap of paper that proclaims that the Hamburg banks will vouch for its full convertibility. And as people know, the world over, Hamburg banks are solid and reliable, and so Hamburg has become the cheapest, most affordable city in Germany...... There is unemployment. Unemployed dock-workers, laid-off sailors and factory workers. A month ago, there was a risk that this great mass of unemployed, cultivated assiduously by communist and nationalist pro-paganda, might spark a revolution or, at the very least, a series of disturbances. And lo! The Hamburg Gold Mark came along, and everything went quiet. It's one of the mysteries of economics why a great mass of hungry people, none of whom had so much as a Hamburg gold pfennig to their name, are pacified by the existence of the Hamburg Gold Mark. Greybeard economists scratch their heads at this wonder. Although no one knows how long it will last."

Added to the economic and financial woes was the prevalent antisemitism. In Roth's essay 'Germany in Winter' he writes:

"In the West End of Berlin, I saw two high school kids. They were walking along the wide, busy road, arm in arm, like a pair of drunks, and singing: 'Down, down, down with the Jewish republic, Filthy Yids, Filthy Yids!'"

Throughout the 1920s, Roth wrote prolifically, travelling inces-santly throughout Europe on assignment, exhibiting nostalgia for losing his original homeland, the Austro-Hungarian Empire, and disillusionment with Germany. He found himself becoming increasingly rejecting of contemporary society, notably Germany and its advancing Nazi party, and of the decision-making of newspaper publishers. Friedrich Nietzsche and Joseph Roth lived at different times, but both shared an increasing distaste for Germany. Nietzsche was born in Germany, yet spent much of his life escaping from it, spending long periods in Italy, particularly Genoa and Turin, and in the mountains of Switzerland, in the village of Sils Maria. Roth, too, welcomed periods away from his adopted city of Berlin during the Weimar Republic. The many forms of crisis-social, economic, political, and cultural- were ever more manifest in Germany in 1930. There was increased censorship, a loss of academic posts and a considerable advance in fascism's future. On 30 January 1933, Hitler officially became the leader of Germany. The Reich President Hindenburg named Adolf Hitler Reich Chancellor. Laws and decrees were swiftly passed, leading to the discrimination, arrest and captivity of political undesirables, above all Jews. Within Roth's work 'What I Saw Reports from Berlin 1920 – 1933' is the report entitled 'The Auto da Fe of the Mind', written in 1933. Within the latter, in a striking passage on the burning of books, Roth writes:

> *"Very few observers anywhere in the world seem to have understood what the Third Reich's burning of books, the expulsion of Jewish writers, and all its other crazy assaults on the intellect actually mean. The technical apotheosis of the barbarians, the terrible march of the mechanised orangutans armed with hand grenades, poison gas, ammonia, nitro-glycerine, with gas masks and aeroplanes, the return of the spiritual (if not the actual) descendants of the Cimbri and Teutoni—this means far*

more than the threatened and terrorised world seems to realise: it must be understood. Let me say loud and clear: The European mind is capitulating. It is capitulating out of weakness, out of sloth, out of apathy, out of lack of imagination (it will be the task of some future generation to establish the reasons for this disgraceful capitulation). Now, as the smoke of our burned books rises into the sky, we German writers of Jewish descent must acknowledge above all that we have been defeated. Let us, who were fighting on the frontline, under the banner of the European mind, let us fulfil the noblest duty of the defeated warrior: let us concede our defeat."

Zweig, too, signalled defeat in his writing, stating in his memoir 'The World of Yesterday':

"I felt that it was more of an honour than a disgrace to share the fate of total literary annihilation in Germany with such eminent contemporaries, including Thomas Mann, Heinrich Mann, Werfel, Freud and Einstein, and many others whose work I regard as far more important than my own."

CHAPTER 8

Displacement of Jews in Europe between 1933 and 1940

To set the scene on the issue of the widespread displacement of Jews in this period, there is Joseph Roth's description of the regime of the Third Reich, recently introduced in 1933, in his 1934 essay entitled 'The Third Reich, a Dependency of Hell on Earth.' The essay can be found in his book 'The Hotel Years.' The title of the essay may well at once capture what Roth intends to be saying, yet the powerful first-hand account in Roth's own words is compelling:

> *"After seventeen months, we are now used to the fact that in Germany, more blood is spilled than the newspapers use printers' ink to report on it. Probably Goebbels, the overlord of German printers' ink, has more dead bodies on the conscience he doesn't have, than he has journalists to do his bidding, which is to silence the great number of these deaths. For we now know that the task of the German press is not to publicise events but to silence them; not only to spread lies but also to suggest them; not just to mislead world opinion – the pathetic remnant of the world that still has an opinion – but also to impose false news on it with a baffling naïveté. Not since this earth first had blood spilled on it has there been a murderer who has washed his bloodstained hands in as much printers' ink. Not since lies were first told in*

this world has a liar had so many powerful loudspeakers at his disposal...."

The intention is to try to convey the scale of the displacement of the Jews in the period 1930-1940. This will mostly be done by citing the direct words of Zweig and Roth as eyewitnesses to such displacement. The passages they wrote will be long but illuminate the enormity of the tragedy. Firstly, though, is a relevant passage from the biography of Walter Benjamin- entitled 'A Critical Life' by Howard Eiland and Michael Jennings- concerning the scale of the displacement in early May 1940 alone:

> *"As the German armies attacked first Belgium and the Netherlands and then France in early May, the French government began a new round of internments. Benjamin – together with Kracauer, the journalist Hanns-Eric Kaminski, and the writer Arthur Koestler – was spared through the renewed intervention of Monnier's friend Henri Hoppenot. But more than 2 million people were now in flight before the Nazi armies."*

Now, we turn to the direct and remarkable testament of Stefan Zweig. In his book, 'Journeys,' Zweig writes a series of essays on travel locations he visited. The essays span between 1902 and 1937. On a lighter note, for a short moment, in his essay on the city of Salzburg in 1935, his settled home for so many years ago, he writes:

> *"Salzburg offers a perfect example of these three elements: earth, water, air."*

There is then, highly reflective of the widespread displacement of Jews, Zweig's travel essay 'The House of a Thousand Fortunes' (written for the 50th anniversary of the Shelter in London). The essay was written in 1937 when Zweig was living in London. Zweig writes, as follows, on the widespread displacement of the Jews during the 1930s before the onset of the 2nd World War:

> *"Today, thousands upon thousands of such people are on the move and amongst them many are Jews. Once again, a terrific hurricane has broken on the world, tearing from the millennial tree its leaves and sending them swirling along the highways of the earth. Yet again, like their fathers and ancestors, a numberless mass of Jews are forced to leave their country, a home where they existed in peace, and find themselves, without most of the time knowing where, another homeland. But in no epoch has the struggle to find sanctuary in a foreign country been as arduous as in the present day, as countries isolate themselves behind hostility and jealousy. Mistrust amongst men has never been so refined, and he who is today a stateless person is disadvantaged as never before."*

The essay then, in particular, concentrates on those seeking refuge at a shelter he describes as 'a house in the East End (of London), in an unremarkable street and yet all distresses have somehow found their way there.' Zweig writes:

> *"The shelter? I had never heard of it, despite residing in London for some time. Never has anyone alerted me to this place, this institution. But the curious thing is that all these Jews coming from the most distant and exotic destinations are fully aware of its existence. In Poland, the Ukraine, Latvia and Bulgaria, from one end of Europe to the other, all the poor Jews know the London shelter. Like the same star seen by numberless people who know nothing of each other, its name represents for them a kind of communion in reassurance. Right across the Jewish*

world, it spreads by word-of-mouth, the legend of the London shelter: somewhere there is a place where the wandering Jew (and how many are obliged now to be so!) can find rest for a weary body and solace for the soul, a place that grants them a few precious days of calm and helps them to continue on their way from one country to another."

As to the length of stay in the Shelter available to those seeking refuge, Zweig writes:

"Naturally, a lengthy stay is not granted to any one of them, for the destitution of the Jewish people today crosses the world like a ceaseless river. Another expelled person will find rest tomorrow in this bed; another will eat at that table: for fifty years, since its foundation, thousands upon thousands have found rest and recovered their strength in the shelter and have left it filled with gratitude. No poet would possess the imagination to paint the diversity and tragedy of these thousands of fates."

Another aspect of the National Socialist regime's cruelty and venom was towards those suffering mental ill-health and dis-ablement. Forced displacement included the movement of hospital patients for the regime's own purposes. This was a very pertinent issue for Joseph Roth, given his wife's severe mental health illness. Roth's book of essays 'On the End of the World' includes a poignant essay entitled 'Poof of Ancestry in the Isolation Cell.' In the latter essay, written in 1938, Roth writes as follows:

"The director of the Berlin office of public health announces that mentally sick patients belonging to the Jewish faith will be interned in asylums strictly reserved for them; under Aryan control, the Jews themselves will run these mad houses."

In relation to the cause of most of the mental health difficulties suffered by Jews at the time, Roth writes:

> *".... It's equally probable that many Jews, following Hitler's seizure of power (and in the immediate aftermath), were literally driven towards insanity. If one ponders the scope and cruelty of Nazi persecutions, of all the regulations and their methods of implementation, of the sadism of the Nordic race clothed in legality and unleashed by the arbitrary, the number of Jewish mental cases seems fairly tame. It would be superfluous to compare it to that mass of people deemed insane who constitute a danger to the public in Germany and are not interned."*

In July 1940, Roth's wife, Friederike Roth, was transferred to the psychiatric hospital of Niedernhart near Linz, where she duly became one of the thousands of victims of the Nazi euthanasia programme.

CHAPTER 9

Zweig, Roth, Benjamin: Their attitudes towards the creation of a Jewish State

ZWEIG AND THEODOR HERZL

When he was a university student, Zweig published his first volume of poetry, and his work appeared in the most illustrious Viennese newspaper of the day, the Neue Freie Presse, whose editor was Theodore Herzl. Zweig first met Herzl in 1901. He developed a warm relationship with Herzl, and Herzl accepted some of Zweig's early essays for publication. In 1894, Herzl had published his seminal paper 'Der Judenstaat' proposing the creation of a homeland for the Jews. Given the sheer misery of Jewish life when this was published, this elegant and simple prescription for the repair of that misery was greeted with open arms and joy by the wider Jewish community. Zweig describes in his memoir that when Herzl's paper was published, he, Zweig, was still at school, and the paper, to him, had the power and forcefulness of a steel bolt. In the several short years of his meteoric career as a Jewish leader, Herzl managed to transform Jewish life and fortune. Herzl's few dozen pages, constituting his written proposal, developed quickly into a mass movement known as Zionism: the Jews would find a new home for themselves in their old homeland of Palestine. Zweig describes in his memoir the general astonishment and annoyance the Herzl proposal aroused in bourgeois Jewish circles in Vienna:

> *"What stupid stuff saying and writing? Why would we want to go to Palestine? We speak German, not Hebrew, our home is in beautiful Austria. Aren't we very well off under good Emperor Franz Joseph? Don't we make a respectable living and enjoy a secure position? Don't we have equal rights, aren't we loyal, established citizens of our beloved Vienna."*

This response, too, would have been expected with such a radical proposal- there ensued a multitude of differing views from Jews in different countries, and Zweig, in his memoir, refers to the Eastern Jews complaining that Herzl understood nothing about the Jewish way of life and was not even conversant with Jewish customs. As for Zweig himself, his response in his own words was:

> *"It was a difficult decision for me to make when I said later (to Herzl), with apparent ingratitude, that I felt I could not join his Zionist movement actively and even help him to lead it, as he had asked."*

Zweig describes how the quarrelsome squabbling and opposition within the movement *"estranged me from a movement that I would willingly have approached with curiosity, if only for Herzl's sake."*

The latter explanation indicates that Zweig never had his heart in the Zionist movement; he was only curious and had some empathy for the idea.

In the Mosaic Magazine article entitled 'Theodor Herzl through the Eyes of a Non-Zionist Contemporary', it says that Zweig wrote about Herzl's proposal:

"This powerful man clearly struck a nerve in the oppressed Jewish masses of the East. He promised them that the hour of redemption was a possibility, and that it could be brought forth through a political rather than a spiritual awakening combined with a single-minded and practical devotion to the cause. But is this not merely Jewish history repeating itself in tragic rhymes? Is not Jewish history replete with examples of leaders who promise the people redemption and lead them only to their ruin? How different really is this Herzl from Shabtai Zvi? Why would this time be any different? The only difference between this failed messiah and the last is that now we have reasonable hopes that the situation of the Jews will improve rather than deteriorate."

According to Amos Elon in his 2002 book 'The Pity of It All', Zweig called Herzl's paper Der Judenstaat 'an obtuse text, a piece of nonsense.'

Zweig saw Herzl many times and describes in his memoir the last time this occurred. Herzl was welcoming and asked Zweig why he had been 'hiding away' from him. Clearly, Herzl bore no grudge against Zweig for the latter's lack of commitment to the movement. Zweig writes in his memoir as to what Herzl said at this last meeting:

"Herzl then spoke very bitterly about Vienna where, he said, he had found most opposition, and if new initiatives had not come from outside, particularly from the East and now from America too, he would have grown weary. What's more, he said, my mistake was to begin too late."

Herzl died at 44, and his funeral was held on 7 July 1904. Zweig was present at the funeral. In an extraordinary passage in his memoir, Zweig describes that day:

"It was a strange day, a day in July, and no one who was there will ever forget it. Suddenly, people arrived at all"

the Viennese railway stations, coming with every train by day and night, from all lands and countries; Western, Eastern, Russian, and Turkish Jews suddenly stormed in, the shock of the news of his death still showing on their faces. You never felt more clearly what their quarrels and talking had veiled over – the leader of a great movement being carried to his grave. It was an endless procession. Suddenly, Vienna realised it was not only a writer, an author of moderate importance, who had died but one of those original thinkers who rose victorious in a country and among its people only at rare intervals. There was uproar in the cemetery itself; too many mourners suddenly poured like a torrent up to his coffin, weeping, howling and screaming in a wild explosion of despair. There was almost raging turmoil; all order failed in the face of a kind of elemental, ecstatic grief. I have never seen anything like it at a funeral before or since. And I could tell for the first time from all this pain, rising in sudden great outbursts the hearts of a crowd a million strong, how much passion and hope this one lonely man had uniquely brought into the world by the force of his ideas."

ROTH

Roth had strong, mixed feelings about everything: his homeland, his Jewishness, his religion, his marriage and love affairs, his friendships, his reputation and indeed, his place in the world. There were two areas upon which he was unwavering. One was his passion and feeling for the vanished Austro-Hungarian Empire. The other was his hatred of nationalism of all kinds, including, in particular, European nationalism. It would follow that Roth would view the idea of a Jewish homeland with disdain. The overall picture, though, points to ambivalence and mixed feelings about this issue, too. Roth was deeply pessimistic about the Jewish future. In March 1933, he wrote to Stefan Zweig that in 50 years, the Jews would no longer exist. He reminded Zweig that they were both fundamentally European and nonreligious:

> *"We come from 'Emancipation' ... rather more than we come out of Egypt."*

In Roth's book "What I Saw: Reports from Berlin 1920 – 1933", there is an article written in 1929 about the Jewish quarter in Berlin called the "Wailing Wall." Within the article, Roth writes:

> *"The Jews are no nation."*

On the other hand, David Mikics, in an Article dated 2 September 2022 entitled 'The Curse of Joseph Roth' for the Tablet magazine, writes:

> *"Roth could be sympathetic to Zionism at times. 'Zionism is the only way out: patriotism, okay, but for one's own land.' But as far as the fate of the Jews was concerned, he inclined toward hopelessness. In June 1932, Roth wrote to Zweig, 'They mean to burn our books, and us along with them.'"*

The idea of a Jewish homeland must have been on Roth's mind when he wrote 'The Radetzky March' since there is an interesting passage in the novel when a character, Count Chojnicki, pronounces:

> *"The monarchy is bound to end. The minute the emperor is dead, we shall splinter into a hundred fragments.... Each nation will set up its own.... little government, even the Jews will proclaim a king in Palestine."*

In his book "The Wandering Jews", Roth further evidences his mixed feelings on the proper identity of the Jewish people and the issue of a homeland for them by posing various questions rather than answering them:

> *"The old questions, the crucial questions, aren't even addressed by the (Russian) revolution: are the Jews a nation like any other, or are they more or less; are they a religious community, a tribal community, or do they merely share certain intellectual features? And is it possible to regard a people that has preserved itself in Europe purely by its religion and its historical separation as a 'people,' and leave religion out of it?"*

Roth firmly and directly, in his own words, answers the question as to his attitude to the establishment of a Jewish State at the very end of his preface to the 1937 edition of his work 'The Wandering Jews.' There, as previously indicated in this book, he squarely says:

> *"Zionism can bring only a partial solution to the Jewish question."*

BENJAMIN

In the summer of 1912, Benjamin was discussing Zionism with a friend, Kurt Tuchler, the founder of the Zionist youth movement, Blau-Weiss. That year, he wrote to a friend about an awakening commitment to Zionism and Zionist activity. Between 1912 and 1913, Benjamin wrote letters to Ludwig Strauss on the "Jewish problem." In 1915, Benjamin first met Gershom Sholem at a youth movement meeting, and from an early age, Sholem had become a committed Zionist. From then on, they remained lifelong friends. Benjamin accepted that he and others possessed a two-sided identity: German and Jewish. Benjamin, however, disagreed with Martin Buber's stance towards Zionism and declined Buber's invitation to write for the journal Der Jude. Benjamin believed that writing was not to be mobilised for political ends. The Bible was of enduring interest to Benjamin, and in the autumn of 1920, he attended classes at the University of Berlin to learn Hebrew grammar for beginners. Sholem emigrated to Palestine in 1923 and encouraged Benjamin, as he had done previously, to come to live there too. However, Benjamin's plans to migrate to Palestine were shelved, and he gave up learning Hebrew. In 1926, Benjamin met the reform Rabbi Judah Magnes in Paris. Magnes was the founder and Chancellor of the Hebrew University of Jerusalem. Emigration to Palestine was a matter Benjamin had grappled with for a long time, yet he made the final decision in 1930 that this was a course he would not pursue. Tensions arose in the relationship between Benjamin and Sholem because Sholem was frustrated and embarrassed by Benjamin's failure to learn Hebrew and come to Palestine.

Joseph Roth in the Place l'Odéon Paris, c.1925. (Bridgeman Images)

Stefan Zweig and Joseph Roth in Ostend, Belgium, 1939.
Photo Imagno/Getty

Stefan Zweig

Walter Benjamin

CHAPTER 10

Benjamin, Roth and Zweig: Forced to Flee into Exile

In his memoir 'The World of Yesterday' Zweig says:

'When the Hitler period began and I left my house, my pleasure in collecting was gone....... I gave part of it to the Viennese National Library when I left, mainly those items that I myself had been given as presents by friends and contemporaries...... I enjoyed creating the collection more than I enjoyed the collection itself. So, I do not mourn for what I have lost. For if there is one new art that we have had to learn, those of us who have been hunted down and forced into exile at a time hostile to all arts and all collections, then it is the art of saying goodbye to everything that was once our pride and joy.'

Zweig, Roth and Benjamin were indeed hunted down and forced into exile. They went into exile to preserve their lives.

As will be described more particularly below, Joseph Roth moved from Berlin to Paris on 30 January 1933; Walter Benjamin too moved from Berlin to Paris soon after, on 17 March 1933; Stefan Zweig moved from Austria to London in 1934.

The circumstances precipitating Benjamin's departure will be set out first, followed by Roth's and Zweig's.

BENJAMIN

In the summer of 1932, Benjamin was nearly at the end of his tether. Professionally, his dreams of academic tenure had evaporated, and he was struggling to make a living as a writer at a time when opportunities for a Jew publishing in Germany were about to dwindle almost to nothing due to Hitler's poisoning of intellectual life.

His personal life, too, was in tatters. Acrimoniously divorced from his wife Dora, estranged from his only child Stefan, and having recently proposed to and been rejected by Olga Parem, a German-Russian woman he desired, he was close to suicide. In a Nice hotel room, he had recently written his will and letters of farewell to some of his dearest friends-he wrote to his former lover, the sculptor Jula Cohn:

"And even now that I am about to die, my life has no greater gifts in its possession than those conferred on it by moments of suffering over you."

Benjamin was still abroad when the National Socialists unseated the left-centre democratic coalition in the German parliament in October 1932. By this time, he had become a well-established literary critic in Germany. In November 1932, Benjamin returned to Berlin, where he witnessed the beginning of the persecution of the opponents of National Socialism. A few of his friends, including Ernst Schoen, the program director of Radio Frankfurt, had already been forced into camps by the end of February; most of the others fled. Kracauer was fired from the Frankfurter Zeitung. Brecht moved to Denmark. The Frankfurt Institute moved to Switzerland. The Literarische Welt closed down. In short, the entire literary and intellectual world on which Benjamin relied and established his reputation was systematically broken and lost in a few months.

Benjamin was exhausted and tired of the struggle for money and his miserable personal life. Once Hitler became chancellor on January 30, 1933, Benjamin understood that his time in Germany was over. For weeks, he barely stepped out of his apartment in Berlin. Benjamin fled the city on March 17, 1933, less than three weeks after the Reichstag Fire. Once in Paris, he searched for a livelihood in what the German communist Willi Münzenberg termed the "capital of the emigration," joining a German émigré community in France whose numbers eventually swelled to more than 30,000. Even with xenophobia rising due to the influx of refugees, Benjamin adjusted rapidly to life in Paris. His French was good, and he had visited the city many times. For the first few years of his exile, he shuttled between Spain, Paris, and Skovbostrand (Brecht's house in Denmark) before settling eventually in Paris. The Nazi regime revoked Benjamin's German passport, and he was stateless.

ROTH

Joseph Roth left Berlin for Paris by train on the very day, 30 January 1933, when Hitler was made Reich Chancellor. 'The Radetsky March,' published four months before Hitler came to power, was one of many so-called 'undesirable' books burnt by Goebbels and his mob. After Hitler acceded to power in 1933, Roth wrote to Zweig in the following explicit terms:

> *"It will have become clear to you now that we are heading for a great catastrophe. Quite apart from our personal situations – our literary and material existence has been wrecked—we are headed for a new war. I wouldn't give*

a heller (penny) for our prospects. The barbarians have taken over. Do not deceive yourself. Hell reigns."

ZWEIG

In his memoir 'The World of Yesterday' Zweig wrote:

"It is difficult to rid yourself, in only a few weeks, of thirty or forty years of private belief that the world is a good place. With our rooted ideas of justice, we believed in the existence of a German, a European, and an international conscience, and we were convinced that a certain degree of inhumanity is sure to self-destruct in the face of humane standards. I am trying to be as honest as possible here, so I must admit that in 1933 and 1934, none of us in Germany and Austria would have contemplated the possibility of one-hundredth part, one-thousandth part of what was about to break over us a little later."

Whilst he did decide of necessity to go into exile, as will be described in more detail below, it remains perplexing that Zweig was showing such naïveté as to the likely forthcoming disaster foreseen by, and warned of, by Roth. After all, not only had Roth explicitly written to him, but Zweig also had written a discerning biography of Nietzsche, which was published in English. Nietzsche died in 1900, yet he was highly insightful in his warnings for the future of Europe. In her book, 'Nietzsche in Turin', Lesley Chamberlain says that Nietzsche was prophetic in detecting a 'destructive germ' in German national identity. Zweig explains that 'destructive germ'—and his naivety as referred to above—in his memoir as follows:

"And perhaps the outside world never understood the real reason why Germany underestimated and made light of Hitler and his increasing power in all those years—not

only has Germany always been a class-conscious country, but within its ideal class hierarchy, it has suffered from a tendency to overrate and idolise the values of higher education. Apart from a few generals, the high offices of the state were filled exclusively by men who had been to university. While Lloyd George in Britain, Garibaldi and Mussolini in Italy and Briand in France had risen to their offices from the ranks of the common people, it was unthinkable for the Germans to contemplate a man who, like Hitler, had not even left school with any qualifications, let alone attended any University, who has slept rough in men's hostels, living a rather shady and still mysterious life at that time, could aspire to the kind of position that had been held by Freiherr von Stein, Bismark and Prince Bulow. More than anything, it was the high value they set on education that led German intellectuals to go on thinking of Hitler as a mere beer hall agitator who could never really be dangerous."

The reality for Zweig was that the years of comfort and eminence ended abruptly with Hitler's rise to power in 1933. Zweig's books were widely denounced and later banned. National Socialists were on the rise, too, in Austria, agitating for union with Germany. Early in 1934, police officers arrived at Zweig's house and demanded to search it for weapons. Zweig packed his bags for London as soon as they had gone, and he never lived in Austria again. In England, Zweig came to discover that a prospective list of persons had been assembled who were to be detained immediately after any conquest of the British Isles by the Nazis, the so-called "Black Book." On page 231 was Zweig's London address. In 1939, Zweig was shocked to be regarded by the British government as an enemy alien. He was able, however, to obtain British citizenship.

CHAPTER 11
Zweig Roth and Benjamin: Their Lives in Exile

All those displaced into exile suffer a crisis of identity and, more often than not, crippling financial hardship. Zweig, Roth, and Benjamin all understandably faced identity crises during their displacements. Roth and Benjamin struggled financially throughout their writing careers, and their displacements could only have exacerbated these difficulties. Although Zweig never suffered financial hardship, the example of his feelings on having to give up his extensive and beloved art collection when he fled Austria, as previously described, is emblematic of the multifarious aspects of loss that must have been suffered by these three writers upon them being unjustifiably uprooted from their homelands, their homes and possessions, from long-standing and familiar family, friends, amenities, and routines. The sense and feelings of isolation were profound. The detrimental effects of such acute, unwarranted disruption must severely damage both physical and psychological well-being. Zweig, Roth, and Benjamin were exiled; they were refugees.

ROTH AND BENJAMIN IN EXILE IN PARIS

Both men's lives were very different in Paris. Roth was familiar with Paris from his time there as a correspondent. It was a favourite city of his. Benjamin was so entranced by the architecture and culture of Paris, including Baudelaire's poetry, that he was intent on pursuing his lengthy Arcades Project. The above said both men had had to uproot themselves from their home city of Berlin and flee.

Roth in Paris

In 1933, Roth uprooted himself from his adoptive city of Berlin and, as previously set out, escaped to Paris on the day that Hitler was appointed Reich Chancellor. He now could not return to Germany, where he was viewed as a vehement opponent of the Nazis. Arriving on 30 January 1933, with Roth were Andrea Manga Bell and her two children with whom he had been living in Berlin. They stayed in Hotel Jacob until March 1933, then moved to the Hotel Foyot, 33 Rue de Tournon. In 1936, he and Manga Bell finally separated. Roth's physical state deteriorated, and, as seen in Roth's work entitled 'On the End of the World', at that time, he wrote to Zweig:

> *"These days, he was surviving on a diet of wine more than schnapps, that he possessed only two suits and six shirts and that he was obliged to wash his own handkerchiefs. He had already spent a large part of the money promised by Zweig and declared a wish to relocate to Brussels where life was cheaper, if he could obtain a Visa."*

Towards the end of Roth's work, 'On the End of the World' is an excellent and detailed chronology of Roth's time in Paris. That chronology is partially drawn from the work 'Joseph Roth in Exile in Paris 1933 to 1939' by Heinz Lunzer and Victoria Lunzer-Talos, 2008. From 1933 onwards, throughout his time in Paris, Roth was always on the move, including visiting Zürich, Vienna, Salzburg and Brussels. Roth was still an Austrian citizen and was entitled to return to Austria to visit. In 1936, through the 'PEN CLUB,' Roth embarked on a series of conferences that took him to Ivov, Warsaw, Vilna, and other cities. From 1936 to 1937, Imgard Keun became a new relationship for Roth. In February 1938, Roth made his final trip to Vienna. On 2 March 1938, Roth left Vienna for good. On 13 March 1938, German troops entered Austria. As for Roth's day-to-day life in Paris, on 25 June 1938, Roth wrote 'A Rest While Viewing the Demolition.' In this short essay contained within his book "Joseph Roth on the End of the World'- he describes himself sitting in the café Tournon, opposite the Hotel Foyot, just off Luxembourg Gardens, which he frequented daily and used almost as an office, watching the Hotel Foyot, his home for so many years, being demolished into rubble before his very eyes, lamenting:

> *"This is the Hotel in which I lived these last 16 years, apart from the time I am on my travels."*

On 11 November 1938, Roth wrote 'In the Bistro after Midnight.' In this short essay contained within his book "Joseph Roth on the End of the World", he describes the Café Tournon as a place *"where I chose to sit each evening past midnight, encountering the so-called little people of the quarter."* In her article "Dead Men in Paris", Monique Charlesworth describes her visit to the Café Tournon and then seeing a blue plaque proclaiming that "The writer Joseph Roth had lived and died in this house in 1939."

His book, The Emperor's Tomb, was published in December 1938. In the spring of 1939, Roth's health deteriorated; he became increasingly depressed about his own and Europe's prospects. On 27 April 1939, Roth secured a contract for his book, The Legend of the Holy Drinker, which was published posthumously in June 1939. Roth died on 27 May 1939.

In May 1940, the Germans invaded France, which rapidly succumbed to the German blitzkrieg.

Benjamin in Paris

In 1933, Benjamin urgently uprooted himself from his home-land of Germany and escaped to Paris. Benjamin was abso-lutely intent on pursuing his lengthy Arcades Project. Over the next seven years, Benjamin built a wide-ranging social network in the French capital. Although they had little con-tact before he relocated to Paris, Benjamin and his cousin, Günther Anders, both shared an intense interest in Franz Kafka's writings and a great respect for Bertholt Brecht. Benjamin visited Brecht, who was exiled to Denmark, during three different summers in the 1930s. In Paris, Benjamin and Anders frequented Paris's cafes and played chess together in the evenings. Anders was married to the philosopher Hannah Arendt, and she and Benjamin developed a strong friendship, which was to endure independently after the breakdown of her marriage to his cousin. He also met the novelist Anna Seghers, like his brother, a communist party member. Beyond fellow refugees, Benjamin established himself amongst the circle of intellectuals around the Collége de Sociologie, such as Georges Bataille, who worked as an archivist and librarian at the Bibliothèque Nationale, where Benjamin did exten-sive research. Benjamin also established ties with Adrienne Monnier, the author and bookseller.

ZWEIG IN EXILE IN ENGLAND AND THEN BRAZIL

Zweig in England

In or around 1934, Zweig urgently uprooted himself from Austria and escaped to England. He abandoned his splendid hilltop home above Salzburg to base himself in London. Friderike was Zweig's first wife, whom he divorced. Zweig and Lotte Altmann met in 1934 when she became his secretary in London. They then became a couple, and their relationship seemed warm and contented. The Zweigs secured British citizenship and, in due course, moved out of London. Three days after the declaration of war on 3 September 1939, they married and made an offer for a house on a steep hill overlooking Bath, much as Zweig's old house had towered above Salzburg.

Zweig had shipped from Salzburg to the UK the first editions of his own works, published in many languages from Croatian to Japanese to Esperanto, housed in the glass-fronted bookcases at their home in Bath. The most personal of them were the first editions signed by Zweig to his young secretary and lover. Zweig wrote optimistically in the first edition of Mary Stuart:

> *"Miss Lotte Altmann, with sincere thanks for her assistance with this and hopefully many other books."*

Zweig in Brazil

Yet again, Zweig uprooted himself and his wife, deciding to depart England for foreign shores. Zweig's depression and Lotte's asthma are generally seen as the root of their deteriorating welfare.

In June 1940, the Zweigs' sailed for the Americas. Lotte explained in a letter:

> *"I am a little worried about him at present, he is depressed, not only because it is really no pleasure to lead such an unsettled life, always waiting what will happen the next day before making another short-term decision, but also*

because the facts of the war, which is now becoming a real
mass murder, and its seeming endlessness weight upon
his mind."

Lotte's ill health manifested itself in endless nocturnal coughing. She was becoming thinner and thinner. A summer spent in New York in 1941 failed to enhance her well-being. It was in this period—since setting off for the Americas—that Benjamin wrote 'The World of Yesterday', which many believe can be easily read as the longest suicide note in literary history.

Though warmly received by the Brazilian government, Zweig never fully settled in his new residence. Zweig wrote in his memoir 'The World of Yesterday':

"Hunted through the rapids of life.... always driven to the
end and obliged to begin again.... comfort had become an
old legend and security a childish dream."

CHAPTER 12
The relationships between Zweig, Roth and Benjamin

ROTH AND ZWEIG

Roth and Zweig were longstanding friends. The depth and longevity of the correspondence between the two men, referenced in more detail later on in this book on the subject of Roth's psychological vulnerabilities, very much reflect this. There was a poignant relationship between the two men. Theirs was a brotherly relationship, too. They were so different, yet so close. The good-natured, polite and well-poised Zweig, on the one hand. The raw, blunt and dissolute Roth, on the other hand. Somehow or other, they complemented each other's distinctly different personalities.

There were understandable commonalities that drove and maintained their friendship. They were literary colleagues, both illustrious writers. They shared a love for and understanding of Jewish culture. They both shared and retained a passion and pride in their former homeland, the Hapsburg Empire, and their lament at its passing. 'Beware of Pity' by Zweig and 'The Radetsky March' by Roth evidence this. They were both very frequent travellers and shared a love or necessity to travel, to be on the move most of the time. In this context, the word 'necessity' connotes that both travelled for professional reasons in their writing and because travelling eased or lessened their restlessness and anxieties while satisfying their unrelenting thirst for knowledge. Zweig's book 'Journeys' is a compelling collection of essays concerning cities he visited. Similarly compelling is Roth's 'The Hotel Years: Wanderings in Europe Between the Wars.'

Despite Roth's and Zweig's commonalities, there were very real differences between them. Roth was clear and prophetic in his early warnings to Zweig and others of the impending catastrophe. Zweig, on the other hand, seemed somewhat in denial of such clear warning signs and, like many other Jews at the time, was prone to bury his head in the sand until the realities became quite evident. Perhaps this was because Zweig had previously led a gilded life, the life of a bourgeois dilettante. There was a deep invisible gulf between Zweig, the assimilated Western Jew born to wealth, and Roth, the poor Eastern Jew from the far frontier of the monarchy. The recipient of a wealthy family, Zweig lived the life of the bourgeoisie; Roth, an alcoholic and almost always penniless, relied on his friend for support. Though Zweig was known to a greater audience, Roth considered himself the better writer, and Zweig knew this. Zweig understood that Roth was an outstanding and brilliant writer and much respected that. Roth often poked fun at Zweig for differing reasons. One was that Zweig's personality was susceptible to this: his naïveté, his good nature, his unshakeable belief in the good of people, his love of humanity, and his wish to be a citizen of the world. Another was that Roth felt he had to make fun of Zweig in self-defence, borne of an effort to retain, and not lose entirely, his self-respect. After all, throughout their friendship, Roth sought and received financial support from Zweig. From Roth's point of view, although he must have welcomed and been grateful to receive monies from Zweig, he may well, at the same time, have resented and felt demeaned by having to ask for and receive such essential support. From Zweig's point of view, it must have been very frustrating for him that, despite his generosity, Roth continued to complain about his circumstances and the world and to drink excessively. One can sense from their correspondence that, with both in exile during the tortuous 1930s, Roth ever more looked to Zweig for financial and emotional support as he became increasingly desperate. All of this complexity in their friendship manifests in the correspondence between the two. Zweig usually offered politeness and respect in his letters to Roth. The raw and blunt nature of the later letters from Roth, on the other hand, typically convey severe irritation and despair:

> *"Don't make me itemise the sorrows that are besetting me"; "Any friendship with me is ruinous. I myself am a wailing wall, if not a heap of rubble"; "Physically, I'm fucked. I've got no money. I owe enormous amounts..."*

In the spring of 1936, for example, Zweig forwarded a considerable number of francs from a Dutch publisher to Roth.

On 31 March 1936, Stefan Zweig, in London, wrote to Joseph Roth as follows:

> *".... You must get it out of your head, the idea that we are somehow being rough with you, or hard on you. Don't forget we are living in a period of general doom, and we can count ourselves lucky if we get through it at all. Don't go accusing publishers, don't blame your friends, don't even beat your own breast, but finally have the courage to admit that however great you are as a writer, in material terms, you're a poor little Jew, almost as poor as seven million others, and are going to have to live like nine-tenths of the human beings in the world, on a small*

footing and with a tightened belt. For me, that would be the only proof of your cleverness: don't always 'fightback,' stop going on about the injustice of it all, don't compare your earnings to those of other writers who don't have a tenth of your talent. Now is your chance to show what you call modesty..."

Although there were many differences between Zweig and Roth, and such complexities too, despite this all, they still seemed, one way or another, to be able to feed off each other intellectually, emotionally, socially and in humour. Through all of this, they maintained their friendship. Speaking of humour, Roth was known, alongside all his challenging behaviours, for his great wittiness, yet Zweig was also quite capable of making fun of Roth. When Roth's book Job—his most Jewish book, a fable of Jewishness- was made into a Hollywood film, 'Sins of Man', it contained no Jews as actors. Zweig mused to Roth:

> *"Your Hollywood-style Job is said to be, well, exquisite.... They've turned Mendel Singer into a Tyrolean peasant.... I simply have to see it. I will roll in the aisles on your behalf!"*

BENJAMIN AND ZWEIG

Benjamin and Zweig never met. They had both separately fled to Switzerland during World War 1. They certainly knew of each other because there was an occasion of professional animosity between the two. When Benjamin's translations of Baudelaire appeared in book form in 1923, prefaced by his essay "The Task of the Translator," they were issued in a minimal edition of 500. They received poor reviews, though some have since become standards in German collections of Baudelaire. Stefan Zweig, then an established figure in the

German-speaking literary world, apparently used the opportunity to further secure his reputation as Baudelaire's German translator by attacking Benjamin. In a letter to Scholem on July 7, 1924, Benjamin wrote:

> *"...the book had been snatched away from the reviewer who had originally been chosen and sent to Zweig, who had published the third-worst German Baudelaire translation fifteen years ago. The review is obviously petty...The person ultimately responsible is the well-meaning, crude, big-mouthed Siegfried called Krakauer."*

Like Roth, Zweig and Benjamin shared a passion for Kafka and Proust. In addition to admiring the works of these highly eminent and significant authors, Zweig and Benjamin also understood the important influence of the Jewish backgrounds of Kafka and Proust on their writing. Both Zweig and Benjamin were polymaths. Although they never met, they interestingly shared an intense passion for collecting, no doubt borne out of their seemingly limitless thirst for learning and understanding various subjects.

As is outlined in 'Three Lives', the biography of Zweig by Oliver Matuschek, Zweig—like Walter Benjamin—was an obsessive collector of historical manuscripts:

> *"Zweig amassed documents featuring the handwriting of Leonardo da Vinci, of Handel and Bach, Mozart and Beethoven, Napoleon, Goethe and Nietzsche, even his and all Europe's nemesis, Hitler. By an imperishable irony, he owned the manuscript on which Haydn set down the notes to the German national anthem."*

Zweig is said to have been so successful that he could afford to buy Beethoven's desk and Goethe's pen.

A zealous collector, Walter Benjamin hunted and purchased books on a staggering array of topics: science fiction, fairy tales and children's books, Judaica, philology, physics, and theology, as well as novels and poetry.

Benjamin and Zweig shared one other bespoke matter in common. Both separately met the poet Rainer Maria Rilke in person. In Esther Leslie's book on Benjamin entitled 'Critical Lives,' she describes how Benjamin came into contact with Rilke:

> *"In the winter semester of 1915/16, Benjamin trans-ferred his studies to Munich.... He was also impressed by a lecture series on ancient Mexican culture and lan-guage, which took place in an elegant private apartment where participants sat on pretty white and black silken chairs around a large table with Persian cloth. Codices were passed around to the handful of people attending, amongst whom was the poet Rainer Maria Rilke."*

Zweig met Rilke on more than one occasion, and indeed, Rilke was one of the extensive networks of friends and acquaint-ances that Zweig could maintain. In his autobiography 'The World of Yesterday' Zweig describes meeting Rilke whilst they were both conscripted in World War 1:

> *"Only with Rainer Maria Rilke did I sometimes have con-versations in which he showed profound understanding. We had managed to get Rilke to come and work for our out of the way War Archive as well. With his over-sensi-tive nervous system, which meant that dirt, smells, and noise caused him actual physical nausea, Rainer would have been a useless soldier. I can never help smiling when I think of him in uniform. One day there was a knock on my door, and there stood a soldier, looking hesitant. Next moment, I started up in alarm. It was Rilke – Rainer Maria Rilke in military disguise! He looks pathetically clumsy, his collar constricting him, upset by the thought of having*

to salute any officer by clicking the heels of his boots. And as in his urge for perfectionism, he wanted to carry out even this pointless formality precisely in accordance with the rules, he was in a state of constant dismay... Luckily, there were helping hands to protect him, and thanks to a kindly medical examiner, he was soon discharged. He came back to my room once in civilian clothes again to say goodbye to me. He wanted to thank me for trying to save his library in Paris where it had been confiscated. For the first time, he no longer looked young; it was as if the idea of the horrors of war had exhausted him.... Then he left, and I was all alone again."

BENJAMIN AND ROTH

Both had separately fled to Paris in 1933. Both were exiled to Paris. They likely crossed paths in Paris, but they were not friends. Benjamin and Roth undoubtedly met in Moscow in the winter of 1926. Roth was visiting the Soviet Union as a journalist that year and saw first-hand the despairing circumstances of the centrally planned economy of communism. As David Mikics writes in his article of 2 September 2022 entitled 'The Curse of Joseph Roth':

> *"The whole Soviet world seemed to Roth a 'monstrous apparatus,' with each person either a bureaucrat, functionary, or worker, and schoolchildren taught a 'banal optimism' that he associated with America. There was no romance in Russia, only lust, a fact reflected in his haunting 1927 novel Flight Without End, where an ardent woman communist seduces the hero and proves devoted to propagandistic debate and bouts of quick sex rather than love."*

Benjamin was visiting Moscow in 1926, around the same time as Roth, having accepted a commission from a journal to travel there to write an article for it. The background purposes for this journey included Benjamin's wish to visit in Moscow the woman Asja Lacis, a Bolshevik Latvian he had met in Capri in 1923. He had visited her in Riga in 1925. As well as that, for a considerable time, Benjamin had harboured socialist/Marxist leanings and no doubt, like many others of the same ilk, he wished to directly observe the ways of the new revolutionary regime in Moscow. Benjamin had previously received a commission to write 300 lines on Goethe from the standpoint of Marxist doctrine for the Great Russian Encyclopaedia. He had been using the language of the left and showing a growing interest in communist politics. Both Benjamin and his long-standing friend Scholem had brothers who were activist Bolsheviks. Benjamin was influenced by Georg Lukacs's "History and Class consciousness." In May 1925, Benjamin wrote to Scholem, saying he would probably accelerate his involvement in Marxist politics, go to Moscow temporarily, and join the party. This all culminated as indicated in Benjamin's travelling to Moscow in December 1926. The trip was financed by a journal co-edited by Martin Buber, which was to publish an account of Benjamin's experiences in post-revolution revolutionary Moscow. Monique Charlesworth, in her article 'Dead Men Meet in Paris' deftly sets out why so many were coming to visit Moscow at the tail end of 1926:

> *".... the winter of 1926, the final winter of literary independence when Stalin was winning the struggle against Trotsky to succeed Lenin and all the long-haired types were in Moscow. The left-leaning intelligentsia of the world met there, from John Reed to Madame Sun, Dorothy Thompson to André Gide, and, of course, a whole raft of German intellectuals, all flirting with Communism and each other in the flesh. Walter Benjamin visited the city and the infinitely tricky Asja Lacis, the woman he had*

fallen in love with two years before—a painful combining
of experiences that stripped many illusions away. And, in
Moscow, Walter Benjamin met Joseph Roth."

Benjamin went to see Lacis, who was suffering from a neural
illness. He held meetings with officials and cultural figures,
including Trotsky's sister. Many illusions about the Soviet
system were stripped away, and years later, in 1934, as
described in Stephen Zacks's 1999 thesis on Walter Benjamin
entitled 'In Memory of Walter Benjamin,':

> *"Benjamin's most explicitly political statement during*
> *his exile was presented as a lecture to the Institute for*
> *the Study of Fascism in 1934, entitled 'The Author as*
> *Producer.' This lecture was implicitly directed against*
> *dogmatic aspects of Soviet criticism as well as against*
> *traditional bourgeois literary history."*

This is how Charlesworth in 'Dead Men Meet in Paris' brilliantly describes the meeting in Moscow between Benjamin
and Roth:

> *"It should not have been a surprise to find them at the*
> *same table, in the same café, as it were: both men were*
> *collecting material for a set of articles which would relay*
> *to Germany what the Russian experience really was. An*
> *excellent journalist, Roth always describes what he sees*
> *and feels; but only here, in the Moscow diary, do we see*
> *Benjamin's thoughts and griefs unmediated. Benjamin*
> *loathed Roth, his lavish hotel suite, his 'face all creased*
> *with wrinkles' which 'had the unpleasant look of a snoop'.*
> *'When I look back over the entire evening, Roth makes a*
> *worse impression on me than he did in Paris,' he wrote,*
> *noting with shuddering distaste that 'Roth had come to*
> *Russia as a (nearly) confirmed Bolshevik and was leaving*
> *it a Royalist'. One might expect two great German Jewish*

writers, both leading lives that were creative yet full of grief, to get on with each other—but they were competitors, I suppose. Unlike fiction, real life is not in the business of deciding whether the endings are going to be happy or not."

Benjamin clearly disapproved of and did not like Roth. It is somewhat ironic that Benjamin said Roth had come to Russia as a nearly confirmed Bolshevik in circumstances where Benjamin himself had materially flirted with the idea of fully becoming a Marxist and joining the Party.

CHAPTER 13

The friendships of Zweig, Roth and Benjamin with others

ZWEIG AND SIGMUND FREUD

Sigmund Schlomo Freud was born on the 6 May 1856. He was the founder of psychoanalysis and lived and worked in Vienna. Freud and Zweig both became internationally well-known and celebrated in their lifetimes. Both were living and working in Austria and would unsurprisingly have come to know each other in such circumstances, yet beyond this, they developed a good, long-standing friendship. Freud and Zweig's friendship continued to the end of Freud's life: Zweig hugely admired the older Freud and developed an amateur passion for psychology; they were both Austrian intellectuals; they were both culturally Jewish. They both lamented the passing of the Austro-Hungarian Empire and spoke about the depressing events unfolding then in Germany. Neither Freud nor Zweig could understand how Germany, with such inspired past figures as Beethoven, Goethe and Kant, was deteriorating in the authoritarian way it was. In his autobiography "The World of Yesterday," Zweig wrote of Freud:

> *"Even Freud, the clearest seeing mind of this time, with whom I often talked in those days, was baffled and could make no sense of the nonsense."*

Zweig sent Freud material he wrote from 1908 onwards, asking his older esteemed friend for feedback. The first piece of work he sent was his play 'Thersites'. As is set out in Dusty Skar's interesting article of the 31 May 2017 entitled 'The Friendship between Sigmund Freud and Stefan Zweig', in 1931, Zweig published "Mental Healers: Mesmer, Eddy and Freud." This was one of the earliest studies of Freud's work by a writer outside the psychoanalytic community. Freud was polite in his reply to Zweig but was not impressed by a work written by an amateur in the field. Freud's book "Moses and Monotheism," published in 1937, suggested that Moses was not Hebrew but a member of the Egyptian nobility. Unsurprisingly, this was not received well by members of the Jewish community in Vienna and elsewhere. It was viewed as antagonistic at a time of suffering for the Jewish people. In 1938 Austria was taken over by the Nazis. The American president, Franklin Roosevelt, wrote to Hitler warning him not to harm Freud. Freud and his family, however, continued to be harassed by the Nazis.

Freud has been referred to as 'The Godless Jew' and was not at all a practising Jew, yet he was at once regarded by the Nazi Regime as of the worst kind to them: he was a Jew and an intellectual. Freud was 83 years old and an invalid. He and his family were forced to make urgent arrangements to leave Vienna. They fled to London in 1938, living at 20 Maresfield Gardens in Hampstead. On 19 July 1938, Zweig visited Freud in London with Salvador Dali. Freud and Zweig talked while Dali sketched. Zweig's last letter to Freud was on 14 September 1939, shortly before Freud died on 23 September 1939. In due course, the Nazis denounced Jewish psychotherapy and seized their assets, including Freud's publishing company.

Referring back to his passionate amateur interest in psychology, Zweig's novel 'Beware of Pity' explores Freudian psychology in differing ways. The young Edith is severely disabled, and in the book, she explores both her severe physical limitations and also the deleterious psychological effects of her disability upon herself and others. Another psychological aspect is the analysis by the doctor in the novel who is treating Edith, Dr Condor, of the nature and extent of his medical duties towards her and her family, to be both candid and honest as to her prognosis yet also encouraging about her medical prospects to maintain their confidence.

As is also set out in Dusty Skar's article of 31 May 2017, Zweig delivered the eulogy at Freud's funeral in Golders Green, an intimate memorial service with a relatively small group of Freud's international allies, among whom were many Central European exiles. It occurred just a few weeks after the British declared war on Germany. Zweig said:

> *"In our youth, we desired nothing more fervently than to lead a heroic life . . . we entertained dreams of meeting such a spiritual hero in the flesh, a hero who would help us better ourselves, a man who was oblivious to the temptations of fame and vanity, who possessed a complete and responsible soul, dedicated to his mission that reaps not its own benefits but enriches all of mankind. Our dear departed Freud fulfilled this enthusiastic dream of our youth. Without Freud's influence, he said, 'each of us would think, judge, feel, more narrowly, less freely, less justly.'"*

ZWEIG AND ROTH'S BAND OF FRIENDS: OSTEND JULY 1936

The summer vacation meeting of émigré refugees in Ostend in July 1936 has become something of a legend partly because it was not simply a holiday meeting arranged between varying friends but was, for all the attendees, a rare and welcome break from the harsh and isolating conditions of exile under the shadow of worsening conditions which were to lead to another world war. Amongst those present in Ostend along with Zweig and Roth were Lotte Altmann, Irmgard Keun, Ernst Toller, Christiane Grautoff, Arthur Koestler, Hermann Kesten, Egon Erwin Kisch, and Willi Muenzenberg. They would mainly all congregate in the Cafe Flore in Ostend. Zweig was residing in a house in the Maison Floreal by the sea. He lived on the fourth floor, Lottee on the fifth. After Zweig and Roth departed Ostend, they never saw each other again.

Lottee Altmann

The introduction of Lotte Altmann into Zweig's life created tensions in the friendship between Zweig and Roth, given Roth's enduring friendship with Friderike, Zweig's first wife. It was all a much-tangled web. Lottee Altmann, who was to become Zweig's second wife, was studying at the University of Frankfurt and had already been denied formal status in Germany in the summer of 1933 because she was Jewish. Her brother was a medical doctor, and from May 1933, he had already been banned from practising medicine in Germany. He and his whole family, including Lotte, came to England, and the brother opened a medical practice in London. As time passed, more and more German émigrés came to him as patients. Although she initially wished to become a librarian, Altmann was offered and accepted the job as secretary to Zweig in London in the spring of 1934. Zweig was 53, and Altmann was 26. On 11 July 1934, Zweig's longstanding friend Joseph Roth and his then partner Andrea Manga Bell went to Nice to meet Zweig and varying other friends. Zweig took Lotte Altmann to Nice with him. Whilst he was there, Zweig's wife

Friderike surprised him by joining them in Nice. It was a painful situation for everyone involved, but his wife was prepared to draw a veil of silence over it all. Roth and Friderike remained close and loyal friends, notwithstanding the increasing disharmony between her and Zweig. Friderika called Roth by the nickname 'Rothi.' Some two years later, when Roth and Zweig met in Ostend in July 1936 together with friends, each and both continued to be having relationship problems. Zweig's marriage to Friderike had finally broken down irretrievably only months earlier, and Lotte Altmann, Zweig's lover, was with him again in Ostend as she was in Nice. As far as Roth was concerned however, this time Andrea Manga Bell was no longer with him because he had recently brought the relationship with her to an end. During his stay in Ostend, Roth learnt the distressing news that Manga Bell had had a nervous breakdown in Belgium. Moreover, Roth was not at all pleased with how Zweig treated Friderike. Zweig's relationship with his wife finally ended upon their divorce, with Zweig and Altmann becoming partners and marrying. Friderike Zweig remained in the family home in Saltzburg, supported by her two daughters from her first marriage, while Zweig was living with Altmann in England and finally with her in Brazil. Friderike and Roth remained very close to the end of his life.

Irmgard Keun

Present within the group on Ostend in July 1936 was Irmgard Keun, who was not Jewish but whose books had been banned in Germany, nonetheless. Her marriage had broken down, her lover Arnold Strauss, a Jewish doctor, had departed abroad shortly after the Nazis took power, and now she had escaped the Nazis. There was an immediate bond between her and Roth in Ostend -they shared the belief that hard drinking was essential to both life and writing. Both were lonely. Only days after their first meeting, Roth moved in with Keun in the Hotel de la Couronne. This helped Roth come to terms with his breakup with Manga Bell.

Egon Erwin Kisch, Willi Muenzenberg and Arthur Koestler

The leading exiled creative minds congregating in Ostend included communists in the fight against European fascism. Amongst them, were Kisch, Muenzenberg and Koestler. Egon Kisch was an exiled Austrian writer and journalist. Muenzenberg is well described in Volcker Weidermann's book 'Summer Before the Dark' as a bear of a man who was the charismatic leader of this circle. Muenzenberg had owned newspapers worldwide, nineteen dailies in Japan alone, and a film production company in Russia. All his German publications and many of those in other countries around the globe were then banned by the Nazis. He was now a leading public face of communism against them. The writer and journalist Arthur Koestler, born in 1905, received money from Muenzenberg to come to Belgium. This he did. Weidermann, in his book, writes of Koestler:

> *"He (Koestler) is already, even now, too independent for the (Communist) party and perhaps also too Jewish. An early convert to Zionism, he moved to the Holy Land, full of enthusiasm, but was soon obliged to sustain himself by selling lemonade in Haifa; rather sobered, he moved back to Berlin, became a reporter for the paper Berliner Zeitung am Mittag, and travelled through the Soviet Union and the Near East; he also flew over Antarctica in an airship. His first big success in book form had occurred two years before, in 1934, with the first volume of his Encyclopaedia of Sexual Knowledge. But now, in exile, he is nonetheless dependent on the (communist) party's goodwill and money."*

Whilst this émigré Communist circle was meeting in Ostend, on 17 July 1936, the fascist leadership of General Francisco Franco rebelled against the democratically elected government of Spain. The Spanish Civil War ensued. There was understandably much frenzy in the discussions between those in the Communist circle in Ostend. Koestler wished to go straight away to Spain, hoping to obtain entry through being a journalist. There was also a very important fresh political event that was troubling Roth at this time in Ostend – on July 11, 1936, Austria signed an agreement with Nazi Germany, which Roth realised was a precursor to the annexation of Austria to Nazi Germany. Arthur Koestler did indeed go to Spain – he succeeded in penetrating Franco's headquarters, was arrested, spent three months on death row, escaped, went to London, repudiated communism, wrote the iconic book Darkness at Noon, and died by joint suicide with his wife Cynthia on March 3, 1983.

Hermann Kesten

Kesten was an influential writer, editor and publisher. Two years before, he had written a horror story set in the midst of a Belgian summer idyll. Roth called Kesten a joker, and as Weidermann writes, *'Kesten had a large stomach and believed that if he just kept sucking it in under the bistro table, no one would notice it.'* After the Second World War, Kesten wrote a book about the world of the émigrés called "My Friends the Poets."

Ernst Toller and Christiane Grautoff

Toller was a Jewish German author, playwright, and Bolshevik revolutionary and an instigator of a revolt against the German government after the conclusion of the First World War. In 1919, he was the leading figure in establishing the "Bavarian

Soviet Republic", of which he became the President and the head of its army. Toller was imprisoned for five years for this rebellion against the central government in Berlin. Whilst in prison, he wrote several plays that gained him international renown. In 1933, Toller, a good friend of Joseph Roth's, was exiled from Germany.

Volker Weidermann, in his book 'Summer Before the Dark', writes:

> *"Finally, the Tollers arrive too, from London, on the direct ship from Dover. Wherever they surface, they are stars, with a nimbus of beauty and fame. The socialist and his goddess, as people call them. The actress Christiane Grautoff is radiantly lovely and unbelievably young. A few days ago, she was still on stage in London as Rachel in Ernst Toller's play 'No More Peace', translated by WH Auden. She received good reviews and was loving her life as an actress in London. Toller is talked about all over Europe as a playwright and champion of revolution. He was the celebrated playwright of the Weimar Republic and the tribune of the Munich Soviet Republic, whose leadership of the revolution cost him five years in jail. He didn't allow it to break him, either in the sweep of his writing or in his fighting revolutionary stance..."*

In due course, Toller joined fellow émigrés in California and then New York. He died by suicide in New York in May 1939, shortly before the death of Joseph Roth. He was 46 years old. The news of Toller's death impacted very heavily on Joseph Roth's health and is accepted to have led to his death in Paris shortly after that of Toller in New York.

BENJAMIN'S BAND OF FRIENDS

Benjamin was able to draw and retain a group of close friends loyal to him: Gershom Scholem, Theodor Adorno, Hannah

Arendt, and Bertolt Brecht. The dynamics between the individuals concerned were tense and difficult at times. Theodor Adorno thought Bertholt Brecht was an unhelpful influence on Benjamin, while Hannah Arendt was deeply mistrustful of Adorno.

Hannah Arendt

Hannah Arendt, born in 1906, was a German-born American historian and political philosopher. She was one of the most influential political theorists of the 20th century. In 1933, the year Hitler came to power, Arendt was arrested and briefly imprisoned by the Gestapo. On release, she fled Germany, settling in Paris. Arendt and Benjamin met in exile in Paris in 1933. Arendt's first husband, Gunter Anders, was Benjamin's distant cousin. As described in the article by Samantha Rosehill entitled "Walter Benjamin's Last Work':

"Arendt, Benjamin and Anders would frequent a café on the rue Soufflot in Paris to talk politics and philosophy with Berthold Brecht and Arnold Zweig."

Despite her first marriage to his distant cousin dissolving, her friendship with Benjamin flourished. During the winter of 1938 – 1939, Benjamin had frequent meetings with Arendt and a circle of German émigrés formed around them. They held regular discussions in Benjamin's apartment. In exile, Arendt had become Benjamin's primary confidante. Meanwhile, Arendt was stripped of her German citizenship in 1937. In 1940-when Germany invaded France - she was detained by the French as an alien and interned. In the middle of June 1940, Arendt escaped the Gurs internment camp, and she went to Lourdes to find Benjamin. After a period together in Lourdes, they went their own ways, and a short while later, Benjamin notified her by writing of his decision to head for Marseille.

On 20 September 1940, Arendt and Benjamin were reunited in Marseille, and Arendt's second husband, Heinrich Blucher, was present. A few days later, Benjamin left for Port Bou. Benjamin handed Arendt a copy of his recently completed 'Theses on the Philosophy of History.' This was Benjamin's final work. As is helpfully set out in the above article by Samantha Rosehill, the 'Theses' were initially written in tiny script on the backs of colourful envelopes—green, yellow, orange, blue, and cream. The stack of empty envelopes on which he wrote his work is now retained in Hannah Arendt's archive at the Library of Congress. Arendt and her husband managed to reach Lisbon, where they boarded the ship SS Guin on 10 May 1941 for New York. They were fortunate in the journey because some two years before, in 1939 - as pointed out in the article "Turning Ourselves into Outlaws" by the Hannah Arendt Centre- the ship St. Louis had meandered around the Atlantic with over 900 German Jews on board, with the United States and Cuba both refusing sanctuary to the refugees. Eventually, the ship had no option but to return to Germany, and most of the passengers on board were ultimately murdered during the Holocaust. Arendt and her husband arrived in New York in May 1941. Their new life in America was to start with the harsh reality that Arendt and her husband were both stateless refugees.

Gershom Scholem

Gershom Scholem, a German-born Israeli philosopher and historian, is widely regarded as the founder of the academic study of the Kabbalah and was appointed the first professor of Jewish mysticism at the Hebrew University of Jerusalem. Scholem was Benjamin's devoted lifelong friend. Their relationship spans from 1913, when Benjamin was 21 and Scholem was 16, to Benjamin's death. They first encountered each other at an event jointly sponsored by the Zionist student group to which Scholem belonged and an organisation for school reform, the Youth Forum. In 1918, Scholem followed Benjamin and his wife and son to Switzerland. Scholem, a committed Zionist, moved to Palestine in 1923 and sought to encourage Benjamin to come to live there too. Benjamin never did. In 1925, Benjamin wrote to Scholem about his dire financial circumstances and said he would probably accelerate his involvement in Marxist politics. They continued to correspond until Benjamin's death. Scholem died on 20 February 1982, shortly after the publication of the English version of the lengthy essay written by him entitled "My Friend Walter Benjamin." It is a fascinating discourse on the lifelong friendship between the two men. Benjamin had long considered Scholem the protector of his career because of the archive of his work that Scholem maintained.

Theodor Adorno

Theodor Adorno, born in 1903 and died in 1969, was a German philosopher, sociologist, psychologist, musicologist and composer. He was a leading member of the Frankfurt School of Critical Theory, whose work has come to be associated with thinkers such as Ernst Bloch, Max Horkheimer, Erich Fromm, Herbert Marcuse, and Walter Benjamin. Adorno has been described as a disciple of Walter Benjamin.

Benjamin and Adorno first became acquainted in Frankfurt in 1923, and their relationship was solidified in 1929 when Benjamin read to Adorno his proposal for a philosophical history of the 19th century, which he contended would retrospectively be referred to as an intellectual watershed for everyone involved. After 1933, when Adorno and Benjamin were forced into exile, their relationship became increasingly close. Adorno provided Benjamin with his only real financial support through the Institute for Social Research, headed by Horkheimer. In 1934, Benjamin began publishing reviews and articles in the journal for social research, using Adorno's intervention. Starting in the summer of 1935, he received a stipend from the Institute for Social Research, which was about one-half of his minimum monthly subsistence. His other publishing opportunities had almost completely dried up. Tensions developed in his relationship with Adorno, who was placed in the supervisor position by the Institute. The difficulty was Benjamin's philosophical history of Paris in the 19th century, which became known as The Arcades Project. His writing on it began to materialise in 1935. In the letter to Adorno that accompanied his synopsis, Benjamin defended himself against Adorno's expressed fear that Bertholt Brecht would be allowed to influence his work. Adorno's response to the synopsis contained nine pages of criticism, yet he prefaced those criticisms with the caveat that he rated the project "extremely high." Their literary disputes continued in the following years concerning the Parisian arcade project.

Bertolt Brecht

Bertolt Brecht was one of the leading playwrights of the 20th century. Benjamin first met Brecht in November 1924 at the home of Asja Lacis, a Latvian Bolshevik whom Benjamin had met in Capri the year before in 1923. Lacis and Benjamin lived together for two months in Berlin in November 1928. At around that time, Benjamin spent much time at Brecht's home discussing art and politics. Through Brecht, Benjamin met the Marxist Karl Korsch. For Benjamin, Brecht represented a new literary type, and he was most excited by

Brecht's literary plays. Brecht and Benjamin planned a new journal, "Crisis and Criticism", to be published monthly. Both men were to edit it with support from several writers: Theodor Adorno, Weill, Bloch, Kurella, Korsch, Marcuse, and Lukacs. The journal was to be political, studying contemporary societal issues, including the 'class struggle.' In early 1931, Benjamin withdrew his association with the journal. This did not impact negatively on the friendship between Benjamin and Brecht. In June 1931, Benjamin spent three weeks in southern France with Brecht and friends. As Esther Leslie, in her book on Benjamin entitled 'Critical Lives', says about that time, discussions between the two men were diverse and lively—Benjamin and Brecht shared their passion for the lives and works of Kafka and Proust. She says:

> *"They discussed Lenin's proposition from 1922 to form 'the international society of materialist friends of the Hegelian dialectic' as well as ideas for a detective play, the trial of Friedrich Schiller and Proust. On another occasion, they mused on Leon Trotsky.... For Brecht, Kafka was 'the only authentic Bolshevist writer.'"*

Following Benjamin's death, Brecht wrote in tribute the poem 'On the Suicide of the Refugee W.B.'

CHAPTER 14

The psychological vulnerabilities of Benjamin, Zweig and Roth

BENJAMIN

Benjamin's crises in Germany from 1930 onwards were personal and professional. He had descended into a deep depression, too. This was not a new occurrence. In his memoir 'A Berlin Childhood Around 1900', Benjamin describes the house from which he came as a *'mausoleum long intended for me.'* In May 1925, he had written to Gershom Scholem, referencing despair over his miserable financial circumstances. All now were standing in the fearful shadow of Hitler's ascendancy to power. Benjamin had endured the final breakdown of his relationship with his wife and estrangement from both her and his son Stefan. He sustained too many blows. His German passport was revoked. There was then announced by the Nazis a ban on foreign travel, restricting such travel to only those people who were able to deposit a large sum of money. He was unable financially to pay that sum. He suffered the blow of the rejection of a book he proposed on Goethe. Benjamin recorded his despair in a journal entitled "Diary from August 7, 1931, to the Day of My Death." He resolved to put to good use his final few days or weeks, having spent many days wondering whether to kill himself in his studio flat or in a hotel:

*"If anything can strengthen still further the determina-
tion, indeed the peace of mind, with which I think of my
intention, it must be the shrewd, dignified use to which
I put my last days or weeks. Those just past leave a lot
to be desired in this respect. Incapable of action, I just
lay on the sofa and read. Frequently, I fell into so deep a
reverie that I forgot to turn the page. I was mainly preoc-
cupied with my plan, with wondering whether or not it
was unavoidable, whether it should best be implemented
here in the studio or back at the hotel, and so on."*

Benjamin did not exercise his plan. In November 1931, he
published an article on the "Destructive Character" in the
Frankfurter Zeitung, consistently alluding to the question
of his suicide. Benjamin ended this short article with the
statement:

*"The destructive character lives from the feeling, not that
life is worth living, but that suicide is not worth the trouble."*

With its immense quotability, the sentence has often been
referred to by those attempting to understand Benjamin's
personality. As already indicated, by the summer of 1932,
Benjamin was nearly at the end of his tether. Professionally,
his dreams of academic tenure had been crushed—he was
struggling to make a living as a writer at the moment when
opportunities for a Jew publishing in Germany were about to
be virtually eliminated.

In June 1932, he had alluded to Scholem that he might take
his life in Nice. He left Ibiza in July 1932 and booked into a hotel
in Nice. He wrote farewell letters. He named Egon Wissing his
executor. Again, he did not follow through. In 1933, he made
the inevitable decision to leave Germany. He determined he
had to move to Paris.

ZWEIG

Zweig was a peripatetic traveller. Hermann Hesse called him the 'Flying Saltzburger.' It was said that wherever you met Zweig, his manner suggested a half-packed suitcase in the next room. His travels included Ostend, Zurich, Calcutta, London, Bath, Moscow, Ossining, Rio, Buenos Aires, and Petropolis. His travels served two purposes. They were a necessary stimulus for his writing. They were also needed in a different way. They eased and lessened his bleak moods and periods of depression. Oliver Matuschek, in his biography of Zweig entitled 'Three Lives', describes the extent to which Zweig's public façade masked a tormented and private self. Depression afflicted Zweig throughout his adult life. Zweig had depression in Salzburg and had asked his first wife to commit suicide with him. In exile in Bath, he wrote that, against the possibility of a German invasion, he had already prepared 'a certain little phial.'

In his work, suicide is everywhere and often closely linked to exile. In 'Twilight,' a novella written when he was still in his twenties, a lady at the court of Louis XV is banished from Versailles and kills herself, unable to tolerate her provincial new life in Normandy. In the unfinished novel 'The Post-Office Girl,' a young woman starts to plan a suicide pact with a disaffected young man after her wealthy relatives briefly treat her to a luxurious life and then drop her. In the short story 'Incident on Lake Geneva,' a Russian soldier, displaced during the First World War and desperate to return home, wades into the lake and drowns. Zweig's demise is a story he has told many times.

'Beware of Pity,' Zweig's only completed novel, is replete with references to suicide. Lieutenant Hofmiller, depressed by his entanglement with the family of the Baron, including in particular the Baron's disabled daughter, the young female character Edith, plans how he will put a gun to his head. He is dissuaded by his colonel from so doing. Edith, pursuant to her rejection by him, commits suicide by jumping off a tower. The Colonel shoots himself during World War I. The latter very basic snapshot of this aspect of the plot should not take away from the beauty and clarity of Zweig's writing in the novel.

ROTH

Roth's wife's severe mental illness, his father's too, and his never knowing his father are all factors contributing to understanding Roth's life and character. Roth wrote of his father:

> *"His speciality was the melancholy which I inherited from him."*

In Roth's essay entitled 'The Strange City' written by him in 1921 and contained within his book 'The Hotel Years', he writes:

> *"One thing is certain: that I am all alone in this strange city...."*

Roth had little or no family support. He resorted to alcohol and became an alcoholic. In a letter to Zweig, his closest friend, Roth wrote:

> *"Never did an alcoholic enjoy his alcohol less than I did. Does an epileptic enjoy his fits? Does a madman enjoy his episodes?"*

'Joseph Roth: A Life in Letters' is a remarkable collection of over 400 letters written and received by Roth over three decades. The dominant correspondence is indeed between Roth and Stefan Zweig. Within his letters, Roth's genius, anger, desperation, and nobility can be seen. They also clearly evidence his psychological vulnerabilities. He wrote:

> *"Don't be upset if my letters are full of impatience and even irritations. It so happens I live and write in a continual state of confusion."*

In a letter dated 1925, Roth wrote:

> *"Nothing ties me... I am not sufficiently sentimental to believe in categories like future, family..."*

In a very stark letter written by him in 1930, he said:

> *"The years I have put behind me are the roads I have travelled... Nowhere, in no parish register or cadastre, is there a record of my name or date of birth. I have no home, aside from being at home in myself."*

By the mid-30s, German publishers could no longer have Jewish names on books. Roth's wife's illness was a constant worry to him as he struggled to pay for her care. He laid bare his desperation at this time in an emotional plea to Stefan Zweig:

> *"I still beg you to continue to think of me as a sensible person subject to occasional fits of madness but broadly in control, and as a conscientious friend who only writes like this in hours of clarity. I have debased and humiliated myself. I have borrowed money from the most impossible places, despising and cursing myself as I did so. And it was all because never in my life have I had anything like a secure financial base, never a bank account or savings. Nothing, nothing, just advances—expenditures, expenditure, advances, and until the Third Reich, I had publishers.... I feel obliged to come before you quite naked, my dear friend. Whatever you do, you cannot judge me more*

harshly than I do myself. I abuse you too, with the desperate selfishness of someone putting the life of his friend in danger by clinging to him like a drowning man clinging to his rescuer.... I have drunk nothing while writing this to you. I am stone-cold sober."

Roth was never always entirely lonely. He, in effect, lost his wife to her serious and long-standing mental illness. His relationships otherwise with women were fragmented. He had a tumultuous affair with Andrea Manga Bell over seven years. From 1936 to 1938, Roth had a romantic relationship with Imgard Keun. They worked and travelled together. As set out in Keiron Pim's biography of Roth entitled 'Endless Flight,' Keun said that Roth had to spend an hour every morning throwing up. She said:

"He's as skinny as a starving child, but his spleen is terribly swollen.... I don't know what's left to love."

Under the heading of an article dated 1st October 2022 written by Philip Hensher and entitled 'The unpleasant truth about Joseph Roth' he says:

"The Radetzky March is an incomparable work, but Roth himself was a liar, sponger and alcoholic who insulted everyone he met."

Hensher was reviewing Keiron Pim's biography of Roth. Certainly, in his last years, in particular, Roth's behaviour deteriorated as he descended into a sea of alcohol. Pim's biography sets out incidents of his bad behaviour and unpleasantness. Stefan Zweig's biography of Friedrich Nietzsche provides a candid and blunt analysis of Nietzsche's characteristics. He writes:

"Nietzsche discomforted them, the eternal outsider in all categories, revolutionary, artist, literary figure,

visionary.... He was a feral savage in his love of the truth....
he made himself poor, solitary and despised in his mis-
sion of integrity.... his spartan will made him inaccessible
and uncompromising.... Nietzsche was in a.... suicidal
conflict with the world."

While there is no intention here to equate their very different
lives and writings, there is a symbiosis between Joseph Roth
and Friedrich Nietzsche in some of the characteristics the
two men shared.

CHAPTER 15

Zweig, Roth and Benjamin: Their Final Journeys

ZWEIG

Zweig died by suicide together with his much younger second wife, Lottie, during the night of February 22, 1942. He was 60, she was 33. Zweig left a letter explaining the suicide pact addressed to Claudio de Souze, president of the P.E.N. Club of Brazil. The letter said:

"Before I depart from life by my own free will, I want to do my last duty, which is to thank this marvellous country – Brazil – which so hospitably received me. Each day I spent here, I loved this country more, and in no other could I have had such hopes for reconstructing my life. After I saw the country of my own language fall, and my spiritual land Europe destroying itself, and I have reached the age of 60, it would require immense strength to reconstruct my life, and my energy is exhausted by long years of peregrination as one without a country. Therefore, I believe it is time to end a life that was dedicated only to spiritual work, considering human liberty and my own as the greatest wealth in the world. I leave an affectionate goodbye to all my friends."

The funeral of the Zweigs is described by Leo Carey in his article of 27 August 2012 entitled 'The Escape Artist: The death and life of Stefan Zweig' as follows:

> *"The day after their bodies were discovered, Stefan and Lotte Zweig were given a state funeral. President Getúlio Vargas attended, along with his ministers of state. Petrópolis shuttered its shops as the cortège passed and deposited Stefan and Lotte in a plot near the mausoleum of Brazil's former royal family. A day or so later, a friend received a farewell letter from Zweig, asking that his burial 'should be as modest and private as possible.'"*

News of the death of Zweig and his wife appeared on the front page of the New York Times on 24 February 1942. On the front page, the headline was: "STEFAN ZWEIG, WIFE END LIVES IN BRAZIL," and underneath, in the front-page column, it said:

> *"Austrian-Born Author Left a Note Saying He Lacked the Strength to Go on."*

ROTH

On the 24 May 1939, Joseph Roth was in the Café Tournon, his habitual drinking haunt in Paris. David Mikics evocatively describes what happened on 24 May 1939 in his article of 2 September 2022 entitled 'The Curse of Joseph Roth':

> *"One day in May 1939, Roth, surrounded by friends at his Parisian café, heard the news that Ernst Toller, another Jewish writer fleeing the Nazis, had hanged himself in New York. Greatly agitated, Roth collapsed and was taken to a charity hospital, the Hôpital Necker. Roth took several days to die in his hospital bed, strapped down by the doctors and screaming for alcohol."*

Alerted by the Hotel Foyot, Friederike Zweig, Blanche Gidon, and Soma Morgenstern accompanied him to the hospital. Roth died at 5.55 am on the 27 May 1939 in the Necker hospital. Philip Hensher, in his article dated 1st October 2022 entitled 'The Unpleasant Truth about Joseph Roth', describes evocatively the sad confusion over Roth's funeral on 30 May 1939 as follows:

"There was no money for a burial in Paris, so that took place on the cheap, in a suburban cemetery where he still lies. Nobody could decide whether he was Jewish or Catholic, or Monarchist or Communist – the representatives of Otto von Habsburg and the Communist Party had an angry confrontation at the funeral. It's somewhat surprising that anyone turned up, given how difficult and unreliable Roth had been to all those who tried to help him...."

Notwithstanding the ignominious burial that had taken place, news soon spread, including internationally, of his death, and his obituary appeared in the New York Times, part of which is set out below:

"Obituary: Joseph Roth, Author of Several Novels by THE NEW YORK TIMES: Joseph Roth, Austrian novelist and journalist, whose opposition to the Hitler regime led him to leave Berlin for Paris in 1933 shortly after Hitler took power, died in Paris...., according to word received yesterday by Dr. Manfred Georg, secretary of the German-American Writers Association, an anti-Nazi group here. Once well-to-do because of his writings, which included the popular and well-reviewed novel "Radetzky March," he had lived in increasingly distressed circumstances in the last few years in Paris and died of tuberculosis after a long illness."

A memorial service was held in London for both Roth and Toller on 22 June 1939. The service is described in the Arts in Exile article entitled 'In Memoriam Joseph Roth and Ernst Toller Programme 1939':

> *"In May 1939, two important exiled literary figures had died within a few days of one another: Ernst Toller on 22 May – by suicide – in New York and Joseph Roth on 27 May in Paris. The Free German League of Culture in Great Britain organised a memorial service for Toller and Roth in London on 22 June 1939. It was the third-ever event held by the League of Culture. It was indeed his longstanding friend Stefan Zweig who gave a speech about the life and work of his friend and colleague Joseph Roth, and he compared emigré artists and writers with the section of a defeated army whose task it is to cover the retreat and allow a realignment to take place later. Despite all the human loss of exile, he was insistent that this task never be lost from view."*

BENJAMIN

In the spring of 1940, Benjamin was released from Clos St Joseph Internment Camp in Nevers and returned to Paris. Benjamin's address in Paris was 10 Rue Dombasle, Paris 15E. He was stateless in France because the Nazis had revoked his German citizenship in 1939. They wanted him because he was a Jew and was viewed as a Marxist. April/May 1940 Benjamin completed his 'Thesis on the Philosophy of History.' As set out in the biography of Benjamin entitled 'A Critical Life' by Howard Eiland and Michael Jennings, Benjamin saw to the safeguarding of most of his important papers/writings to Georges Bataille, Greta Adorno and Hannah Arendt. Around 14 June 1940, Benjamin and his sister Dora left Paris by train to Lourdes just a day before the Germans entered the capital with orders to arrest him at his flat. They spent approximately two months there. As related elsewhere in this book, Hannah Arendt escaped from the Gur internment camp in the middle of June 1940 and hastened to Lourdes to find Benjamin. There, they met up. In mid-August 1940, Benjamin departed for Marseille whilst his sister Dora remained in Lourdes. In Marseille, Benjamin collected his papers for emigration. Max Horkheimer, the German philosopher and sociologist, had assisted Benjamin in securing this. On 20 September 1940, Benjamin and Hannah Arendt were reunited in Marseille. In late September 1940, Benjamin, with the photographer Henny Gurland (the wife of Eric Fromm, the German social psychologist and psychoanalyst) and her son Joseph, took the train from Marseille into the countryside near the Spanish border.

From this countryside, Benjamin's escape on foot from occupied France began on Tuesday, 24 September 1940. That day, the group he was with (which included Lisa Fittko, a smuggler of refugees, and Gurland and her son) went on a reconnaissance practice run, but unlike his fellow refugees, Benjamin did not go back at the end of the day. Instead, he stayed the night at a crossroads and waited for the others to return. This was because of his exhaustion. The next day, Wednesday, 25 September 1940, the group trekked through the treacherous mountain pass route from Banyuls in France to the Spanish town of Port Bou. This journey involved several hours of climbing a mountain on a scorching September day, and clearly, Benjamin was exhausted and near the end of his tether. He had a heart condition. He was carrying a leather attaché case, and the mystery of what the case contained remains. At the mountain's summit, Fittko's group, including Benjamin, met another group of refugees led by Austrian smuggler Carina Birman. The group reached the railway station at Port Bou on 25 September, only to be informed by the Spanish authorities that they had entered Spain illegally, would be held overnight in a local hotel and sent back to occupied France the next morning. Birman has said that she spoke to Benjamin in his room and that he said he would not leave the hotel and could not make it back to the border. She also said that he had inferred he had some sort of poison in pill form. In any event, Benjamin must have been physically exhausted and emotionally devastated by the circumstances he found himself in. There is no dispute that Benjamin died by suicide. He is said to have swallowed morphine pills in his hotel room in Port Bou. As is set out in the biography of Benjamin entitled 'A Critical Life' by Howard Elland and Michael Jennings, Benjamin had been speaking to the distinguished writer Arthur Koestler in Marseille (before embarking on his journey to the French-Spanish border) and had confided to him that he held enough morphine 'to kill a horse.' Koestler was also amongst those trying to get out of France.

Even though Hannah Arendt wrote to Gershom Scholem that Benjamin died on 29 September- she (Arendt) was not one of those present at Port Bou at the time—it is generally otherwise accepted that Benjamin died on Thursday, 26 September 1940. Yet, there is still controversy as to the time of his death. Port Bou documents put the official time of death as 10 pm on 26 September, yet the accounts of Henny Gurland and Carina Birman-who were present at Port Bou at the time- are that they were informed of his death on the morning of 26 September.

Henny Gurland maintained that Benjamin had left her a note to be imparted to Theodor Adorno, which she committed to memory and then destroyed as a precaution. When in the USA, she relayed to Adorno that the note had said:

> *"In a situation that leaves no way out, I have no choice other than to end this."*

There is no doubt that Benjamin was buried in the Catholic section of the cemetery at Port Bou. He was not buried under his actual name but as Benjamin Walter. There remains speculation as to why this was so. Catholic burials were forbidden in cases of suicide, and this may be why the Spanish doctor's death certificate declared Benjamin had died from a cerebral haemorrhage on 26 September. There remains controversy on the exact date of his burial, too. The records kept by the municipal government of Port Bou and church records differ: the municipal certificate shows that he was buried on 27 September; another burial record gives the date as 28 September.

There is a terrible irony in Benjamin having chosen to end his life on 26 September 1940, as he did, because the remaining group of refugees who, like him, had been refused entry into Spain, were taken back to the border where the authorities changed their decision – they were permitted to enter Spain. As is raised in the article of 9 July 2012, 'Chronicling Walter Benjamin's Final Hours' by Noa Limone, there can only be speculation as to why there was such a change of view by the authorities: was it because a bribe was accepted? Were they allowed entry because Benjamin was no longer with them? Or was it an act of sympathy/humanity to the remaining group in light of Benjamin's suicide? The journey made by Benjamin to the border, the contents of the leather attaché case he was carrying, his attempt to leave France, and his very tragic demise all remain a constant source of dramatic interest, with the contentious details referred to above likely to be forever unresolved. Benjamin has left us too with the very sombre words of warning within his last written work 'Theses on the Philosophy of History':

> *"Only that historian will have the gift of fanning the spark of hope in the past who is firmly convinced that even the dead will not be safe from the enemy if he wins."*

CHAPTER 16
Zweig, Roth and Benjamin: A Reflective Overview

How does anyone cope with displacement from their homeland or permanent exile through war? Roth describes in his own words the emotions of despair for those displaced in his preface to the 1937 edition of his work 'The Wandering Jews':

> "In such a world, not only is it out of the question that émigrés should be offered bread and work but it is taken for granted. It has also become out of the question for them to be issued so-called papers. What is a man without papers? Rather less, let me tell you, than papers without a man!"

In Hannah Arendt's seminal essay 'We Refugees' she writes:

> "Our optimism, indeed, is admirable, even if we say so ourselves. The story of our struggle has finally become known. We lost our home, which means the familiarity of daily life. We lost our occupation, which means the confidence that we are of some use in this world. We lost our language, which means the naturalness of reactions, the simplicity of gestures, the unaffected expression of feelings. We left our relatives in the Polish ghettos and our best friends have been killed in concentration camps, and that means the rupture of our private lives."

Whatever the terminology- refugee, immigrant, asylum seeker, wherever in the world the escape is from—the dilemma for the person seeking refuge and safety, to use Arendt's words, is 'If I am saved, I feel humiliated, and if I am helped, I feel degraded.' It was not just Zweig, Roth and Benjamin as Jewish intellectuals- Bertholt Brecht and Thomas Mann, as examples only, were not Jews, and they too were intellectuals displaced into forced exile in 1933 assisted by the writer Hermann Hesse, whose third wife was Jewish. In the late 1930s, German journals stopped publishing Hesse's works, and the Nazis eventually banned them. Hesse, Brecht, Arendt, Adorno, Scholem, Schoenberg and others managed to survive the inferno and go on to live fruitful lives. Zweig, Roth and Benjamin did not. Nor did Ernst Toller, whose suicide occurred shortly before Roth's death. Koestler appeared to have overcome the inferno, only to become lost to suicide later on, in 1983. Immediate relatives perished, too: Walter Benjamin's brother Georg perished in the Mauthausen concentration camp, and Joseph Roth's wife died under the Nazi euthanasia programme for the mentally ill. Imagine for a moment Marseilles in September 1940, the chaos, the panic, with thousands upon thousands of persons trying to flee—amongst the throngs were Walter Benjamin, Hannah Arendt and Arthur Koestler. Koestler is the one discernible literary figure to meet all three of the subjects of this book: Zweig, Roth and Benjamin. He spoke to Benjamin in Marseille in September 1940. He met Zweig and Roth in Ostend in 1936. Zweig, Benjamin and Roth were brilliant men of letters. The three of them were excellent writers, intellectuals and secular Jews. They were restless and anxious men. They were peripatetic travellers. Roth's childhood was marred by his never having known his father, who had a mental illness, as was also the case with Roth's wife. Her mental illness was severe and long-standing. Benjamin, too, wrote about an unhappy childhood. In his book 'A Berlin Childhood Around 1900' Benjamin describes the house from which he came as a 'mausoleum long intended for me.' There is no suggestion in Zweig's case of an unhappy childhood, yet he and Benjamin both suffered from mental health vulnerabilities throughout their lives. Thoughts of suicide were present at varying points in their lives. The reasons for Roth's severe alcohol abuse lay rooted in the unhappiness of his childhood. All three men died by suicide, and included here is Roth—whilst he technically died of pneumonia, it is generally accepted that he willed himself to death through his severe abuse of alcohol and personal self-neglect. The above said, it must be noted that all three (Zweig, Roth and Benjamin) valued their lives very much, as reflected by the steps they took to avoid serving on the front line in World War I. They wished to stay alive. Roth and Zweig served in military capacities that avoided them being in danger of death or serious injury. Benjamin avoided military service altogether. Fast forward to 1939/40, both Roth and Benjamin obtained papers authorising their emigration to America, indicating they had still not completely lost the will to survive. Benjamin was still trying to escape to safety on his journey across the Pyrenees. Zweig was able to reside in Brazil, a country of safety. No one can ever fully know why a person dies by suicide. Yet, it would not be remarkable to consider the depth, breadth and severity of the personal, psychological, political and economic pressures that must have borne down on all three men. Each and all of them lived through and experienced the totemic changes brought about by the disaster of the First World War. Roth and Zweig lamented the loss of their homeland, the Austro-Hungarian Empire. As was the case for millions of others, Zweig, Roth and Benjamin had to rebuild their lives from the debris of that conflagration. It would not be uncommon at any time for writers to sustain financial uncertainty. Roth and Benjamin suffered financial difficulties throughout their careers. Zweig not so because of his wealthy background. Zweig, in particular, became known between the two world wars as a highly successful writer, both nationally and internationally. Yet all three men had, in addition, unjustly foisted upon them virulent hatred because of two factors: they were Jews, and they were intellectuals. The flavour of the intensity of the increasing instability of the Weimar Republic is evidenced by the assassination in 1922 of Walter Rathenau, the Jewish foreign minister of Germany, and by Joseph Roth's direct observations in his essays 'What I Saw Reports from Berlin 1920-33.' Hunger, chaos, economic and political instability, inflation, and increasingly nationalistic far-right activity and anti-Semitism were all prevalent. Zweig was somewhat insulated from all of this, living as he did in his comfortable home in Salzburg, seemingly protected by his worldwide reputation. He, too, however, was not able to escape the consequences of being a Jew and an intellectual. His literature was banned and burned by the Nazi regime, as was the case with the works of Roth and Benjamin. Alongside this, Zweig, Roth and Benjamin could not sustain anything but fragmented and insecure relationships with partners. Zweig was married to his first wife for a lengthy period that endured while they lived in Salzburg, but the marriage deteriorated and broke down irretrievably. Zweig fled to London in 1934 and remarried whilst in England. Roth's wife remained in a sanatorium, suffering from severe mental illness, and he thereafter had several relationships with other women. Benjamin became estranged from his wife and son, and he and his wife divorced. The point is not to seek to untangle precise reasons for their lives coming to a premature end but to try to understand all the displacements Zweig, Roth, and Benjamin suffered. Having lived through and survived

World War I, all three must have pinched themselves in disbelief and despair at the thought that there would likely be a Second World War conflagration. Regarding displacement, Roth and Zweig had already lamented the loss of their beloved homeland, the Austro-Hungarian Empire. Now, the three of them were forced to flee in the knowledge that they were likely otherwise to be captured, imprisoned and killed. Apart from his frequent travelling in order both to write and to lessen his depressive moods, Zweig had spent the whole of his life in Austria and, for many years, was settled in Salzburg. He had to leave this all behind in 1934 after fascists searched his property. Even in exile in England, he knew he was not safe. He was on a list of exiles who would be arrested upon the Gestapo reaching London. This culminated in his further unhappy exile to Brazil. Both Roth and Benjamin had had to flee Berlin in 1933 for Paris. Benjamin undoubtedly loved Paris and its Arcades, which became his real home. Yet again, he had to flee his apartment in Paris in 1939, shortly before fascists raided it. One can only imagine Benjamin's exquisite collection of artefacts and furniture in his apartment. This had to be abandoned at short notice, and his life and home were gone. Roth never really had a residence of his own, living as he did in Paris, mostly in a hotel, and he too would likely have been arrested, imprisoned and killed had he not died in Paris in the way he did. For him, the loss of his friend Ernst Toller by suicide was too much. What is striking is that whilst, on the one hand, throughout the 1920s, the Weimar Republic was tottering and crumbling, on the other hand, there was a positive flood of intellectual and artistic creativity. There was the legacy of the works of Proust and Kafka, who died in the early 1920s. Alongside Roth, Zweig and Benjamin, there was a rich tapestry of other writers: Sigmund Freud, Arthur Koestler, Thomas Mann, Hermann Hesse, Hannah Arendt, Theodor Adorno and

Rainer Maria Rilke. Another positive feature in an otherwise bleak background was how friendships proved important to the three men. Zweig and Roth sought to support each other as long-standing friends, particularly in the tortuous 1930s. Benjamin was closeted in close friendships with Scholem, Adorno, Arendt, and Brecht. Zweig and Roth both enjoyed the warmth of the group of their friends who assembled in Ostend in 1936, including Ernst Toller and Arthur Koestler.

Zweig, Roth, and Benjamin should not be grouped together as one entity. They were very different and distinct individuals who had much in common. The three men never met in person, and accordingly, there is no photograph of them together. What were they like as individual characters?

Zweig was a reserved and refined man of letters, accustomed to a bourgeois lifestyle and with no money worries. He was a polymathic intellectual who was restless and travelled frequently to both write and ease his depressive moods. He may be described euphemistically as 'the peripatetic traveller.' He could, at times, be viewed as somewhat flamboyant. Yet, besides being an excellent writer and collector, Zweig was a brilliant self-publicist who managed to network with 'the great and the good' and establish himself as a nationally and internationally known writer. He maintained friendships with Sigmund Freud, Theodor Herzl and Joseph Roth. He was present at Herzl's funeral. He was the principal speaker at Freud's funeral and Roth's memorial in London in 1939. Recently, there has been a marked and deserved renaissance of appreciation for the breadth and depth of Zweig's excellent writing.

Roth came to sadly live a spartan, rootless and dissolute life overborne by alcohol, rooted, as indicated, in his unhappy childhood but also exacerbated by the persecution and displacement he had to endure. Nor was he able to achieve any long-lasting and secure personal relationships.

Although Roth never divorced his wife, it was never a substantive relationship because of her longstanding severe mental illness. Roth's positive characteristics are manifest. He was raw, straightforward and blunt with others, sometimes offensive, but he always sought to say it as it was. He wore his heart on his sleeves. Despite his other negative characteristics, his biting wit and humour enabled him to endear himself to others. Financial difficulties consistently burdened him, and he frequently travelled too, which arose from his journalism career. Roth may be described euphemistically as 'the peripatetic correspondent'. Beyond all of the above, Roth was not only a brilliant and acclaimed writer, including classic novels, but he was also insightful, prophetic, and politically attuned, warning from early on of the dangers to come. Roth understood at an early stage the seismic changes yet to be unleashed on the world and the likely outcome for the Jews.

Benjamin was a highly academic and polymathic intellectual. He was also a solitary, reserved, and restless man. He, too, was a frequent traveller for the same reasons as Zweig. He suffered bouts of severe anxiety. He was beset by financial difficulties throughout his life. His ideas, interests and writing were eclectic and wide-ranging, and his quest for knowledge was relentless and unceasing. He may be described euphemistically as 'the peripatetic student'. Benjamin could, at times, be highly polemic and critical of the works of other writers, and many in the academic and literary establishment found his writing and views too challenging and unsettling. This is likely why Benjamin could not achieve the academic university professorship that might have been ideal for him. Benjamin was 'one of a kind' or, as Hannah Arendt deftly put it, he was 'sui generis'. Since his death, Benjamin has become increasingly acclaimed as somewhat of an intellectual cult figure- a writer, thinker and philosopher ahead of his time in the disparate subjects he wrote about, including the dimensions of nascent modern media and culture.

The lives of displacement suffered by Zweig, Roth and Benjamin and their tragic demise speak to millions of other innocent victims who were not eminent writers and who, in differing ways, suffered the same fate as them.

Epilogue

Zweig, Roth and Benjamin were three innocent individuals who happened to be eminent writers. That they were secular Jews who were not actively observant religiously was irrelevant to the Nazi regime. Their professional accomplishments, too, were to mean nothing in the end to fascism except one reason for persecution. As both Jews and prominent intellectuals, they were ripe prey for the National Socialists. One way or the other, none of the three could escape paying the ultimate price. Their will to live – so forceful when they sought to avoid injury and death in World War I, still so actively alive as they fled into exile – evaporated under the pressures of displacement and persecution.

Notwithstanding their high intellects, all three men demonstrated significant human vulnerabilities, and these characteristics contributed to the brilliance of their writing. Although they left this world in fear of capture and death, at the same time, they have left with us the rich legacy of their writing, imagination and ideas. The tragic premature unravelling of the lives of these three men has also bequeathed us the opportunity to seek to understand the meaning and feelings of exile and displacement for those souls simply seeking security and safety from oppression.

The lives of Stefan Zweig, Joseph Roth and Walter Benjamin were cut short by sheer evil. *Three eminent writers hunted to death by fascism.*

Dedication

The inspiration for this book 'DISPLACEMENT' comes from the short life and work of Alexander Ulrich Boschwitz. He was a young man who wrote a brilliant novel called 'The Passenger' exploring the fictional life of a Jewish businessman, Otto Silbermann, who had to leave his apartment in Berlin and 'go on the run' to escape Nazi capture. The narrative is set in November 1938. The story encapsulates the sheer terror involved in trying to avoid capture and the utter disturbing chaos involved in doing so. It is a story of displacement. The outcome for the main character shall be left unsaid. Yet, beyond the novel was the real-life tragedy of the author Boschwitz himself, whose father was Jewish by origin and mother not so.

In 1935, Boschwitz and his mother escaped Germany following the promulgation of the Nuremberg Laws, and he (Boschwitz) moved from Sweden to France, Luxembourg, and then to Belgium before joining his mother in England. Boschwitz wrote the novel in London over a very short period of three weeks. Despite hoping for safety on these shores, the British Government pronounced him an 'enemy alien', and Boschwitz was interned following the outbreak of hostilities in a camp on the Isle of Man, along with thousands of other refugees from Germany and Austria. He was then peremptorily deported by the British

Government to Australia. There, he was interned in a prison camp in New South Wales. In due course, the British government granted permission for him and other refugees to be returned to England; however, on the ship bringing him and the others back to England in 1942, disaster struck – the Germans bombed the ship, and Boschwitz was killed along with 361 others. He was 27 years of age. Some 70-plus years after his death, the original German typescript of 'The Passenger' turned up in an archive in Frankfurt. The novel finally appeared in its original language in 2018.

This book, DISPLACEMENT, is dedicated to the memory of Ulrich Alexander Boschwitz and to the millions of other innocents who suffered similar fates to him.

Acknowledgements

I am hugely grateful to Sandra David of Arrow Gate for believing in me and my work and for her inspirational leadership in bringing DISPLACEMENT to publication alongside all the hard work and expertise of her colleagues.

Beyond all else, my thanks go to my wife Amanda and our three children, Rebecca, Rupert and Thomas, for all their unwavering encouragement, love and support together with Max, Rina, Snow, Dorrie, Harriet, Andreas and Janet.

Bibliography

Arendt, H. (2005) *Responsibility and Judgment*. New York: Schocken Books.

Arendt, H. (2008) *The Jewish Writings*. New York: Schocken Books.

Arendt, H. (1943) 'We Refugees', in *The Jewish Writings*. New York: Schocken Books.

Benjamin, W. (2006) *Berlin Childhood around 1900*. Cambridge: The Belknap Press.

Benjamin, W. (2015) *Berlin Chronicle*. New York: Studio Hudson.

Benjamin, W. (1992) *Illuminations*. London: Fontana Press.

Benjamin, W. (2009) *One Way Street and Other Writings*. London: Penguin Books.

Benjamin, W. (2002) *The Arcades Project*. Cambridge: Harvard University Press.

Boschwitz, U.A. (2021) *The Passenger*. London: Pushkin Press.

Britt, B. (2015) 'Benjamin's displaced Jewish tradition', in Lebovic, N. (ed.) *The Future of Benjamin, 7+2 Articles*.

Boylan, R. (2012) 'A March to the Grave Joseph Roth and the End of the Austro-Hungarian Empire', *Arts in Society*, 1 November.

Carey, L. (2012) 'The Escape Artist: The Death and Life of Stefan Zweig', *A Critic At Large*, 20 August.

Chamberlain, L. (2022) *Nietzsche in Turin*. London: Pushkin Press.

Eiland, H. and Jennings, M. (2014) *A Critical Life*. Cambridge: Harvard University Press.

Hill, S.R. (2019) 'Walter Benjamin's Last Work', *Los Angeles Reviews of Books*, 9 December.

Jay, M. (1999) 'Walter Benjamin, Remembrance, and the First World War', *Review of Japanese Culture and Society*, December.

Jeffries, S. (2014) 'Walter Benjamin: A Critical Life review-gambler, womaniser, Thinker', *The Guardian*, 7 August.

Kamm, O. (2021) 'Proust's Jewish identity is too often overlooked', *The Jewish Chronicle*, 18 February.

Kirsch, A. (2014) 'One of Liberalism's Greatest Defenders Doesn't Deserve His Obscurity-the pathos of Stefan Zweig and his overdue revival', 9 August.

Kirsch, A. (2016) 'Stefan Zweig and Joseph Roth-How Europe's exiled intellectuals ended up on a Belgian beach', *New Statesman*, 25 January.

Larsen, E. (n.d.) 'Critique of "The Work of Art in the Age of Mechanical Reproduction"'. New Haven: Yale University Press.

Leslie, E. (2007) *Critical Lives Walter Benjamin*. London: Reaktion Books.

Lunzer, H. and Lunzer-Talos, V. (2008) 'Joseph Roth in Exile in Paris 1933 to 1939'.

Matuschek, O. (2013) *Three Lives*. London: Pushkin Press.

Mauk, B. (2014) 'Hannah Arendt was right: Walter Benjamin is 'sui generis'', *Salon*, 19 March.

Phillips, F. (2015) 'Why did Stefan Zweig choose suicide when he had the chance of a new life in exile?', *Catholic Herald*, 22 January.

Pim, K. (2023) *Endless Flight*. London: Granta Publications.

Prochnik, G. (2015) *The Impossible Exile: Stefan Zweig at the End of the World*. London: Granta Books.

Pulzer, P. (1964) *The Rise of Political Antisemitism in Germany and Austria*.

Rees, J. (2017) 'The Private Life of Stefan Zweig in England', 9 February.

Rivas Molina, F. (2023) 'Nueva Germania, the Aryan utopia of Nietzsche's sister and Bernhard Forster in Paraguay', *El Pais International*, 9 May.

Roth, J. (2013) *JOB: The story of a simple man*. London: Granta Books.

Roth, J. (2019) *On the end of the world*. London: Pushkin Press.

Roth, J. (2016) *The Hotel Years*. London: Granta Books.

Roth, J. (2022) *The Radetzky March*. London: Granta Books.

Roth, J. (2013) *The Wandering Jews*. London: Granta Publications.

Roth, J. (2011) *What I Saw Reports from Berlin 1920-1933*. London: Granta Books.

Scholem, G. (1981) 'My Friend Walter Benjamin', *Politics and Ideas*, December.

Skar, D. (2017) 'The friendship between Sigmund Freud and Stefan Zweig', 31 May.

Stern, F. (2000) *Einstein's German World*. London: Allen Lane The Penguin Press.

Weidermann, V. (2016) *Summer Before the Dark*. London: Pushkin Press.

Wistrich, R. (1990) *The Jews of Vienna in the Age of Franz Joseph*. Liverpool: The Littman Library of Jewish Civilization in association with Liverpool University Press.

Zacks, S. (2001) 'Walter Benjamin: To the Memory of Walter Benjamin', Thesis, Liberal Studies, New School for Social Research, The New School Archives, New York.

Zweig, S. (2024) *Beware of Pity*. London: Penguin Classics.

Zweig, S. (2019) *Journeys*. London: Pushkin Press.

Zweig, S. (2020) *Nietzsche*. London: Pushkin Press.

Zweig, S. (2021) *The Royal Game and Other Stories*. London: Pushkin Press.

Zweig, S. (2024) *Six Stories*. London: Penguin Books.

Zweig, S. (2009) *The World of Yesterday*. London: Pushkin Press.

Index

About the Author

Having studied law at Magdalen College Oxford, Richard Harper practised as a barrister and then sat as a family law judge. During his judicial career he has written on medical treatment and the law relating to the protection of children and vulnerable adults. He now writes and lectures on the overall law relating to the protection of children, and DISPLACEMENT is his first work of nonfiction outside of the law. The connecting theme of Harper's writing is examining injustice and how it may be ameliorated. He lives with his family in West London.